DAILY BLESSINGS

FOR MY

Husband

HONOR BOOKS

Daily Blessings for My Husband
ISBN: 979-8-88898-142-9 - *Paperback*
ISBN: 979-8-88898-143-6 - *Hardcover*
ISBN: 979-8-88898-144-3 - *Ebook*

Copyright © 2024 by Honor Books
Racine, WI

Cover Design by Faille Schmitz.
Manuscript written by Melody Carlson.

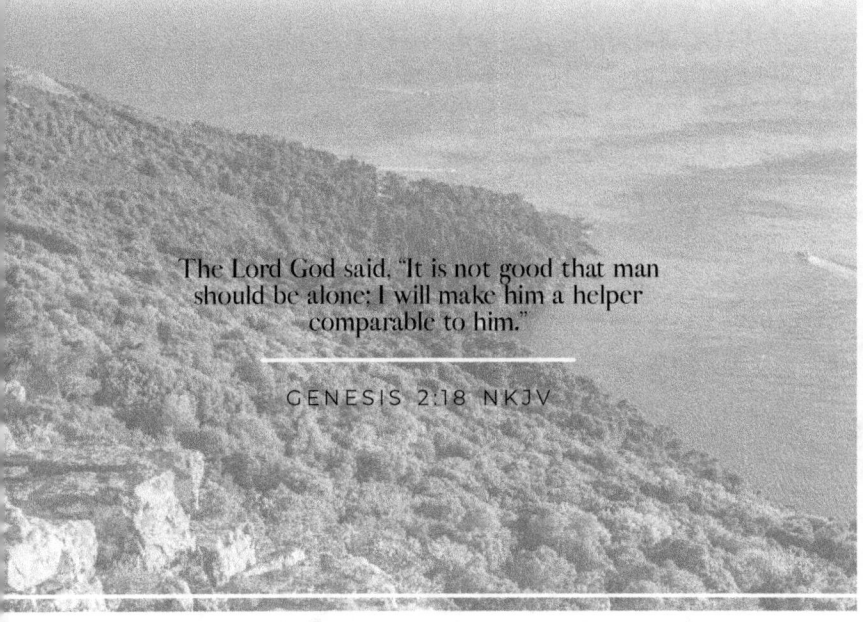

The Lord God said, "It is not good that man should be alone; I will make him a helper comparable to him."

GENESIS 2:18 NKJV

My Dear Husband,

Our love is one of life's greatest blessings. I want you to know how much you mean to me—how much I love you. And I want to assure you that I believe in our marriage. I long for the two of us to grow closer and more in love than ever before.

But sometimes it's difficult to put such heartfelt feelings into words.

And so, I hope this little book will communicate my deepest thoughts and desires for you and for our relationship. And as you read these simple words each day, I hope that you will receive them as a gift from my heart to yours.

Because I love you,

Your Wife

I Choose to Love You

Dear friends, let us love one another, for
love comes from God. Everyone who loves
has been born of God and knows God.

1 JOHN 4:7 NIV

My Dear Husband,

I bless you with my heartfelt love. I want you to know that I am committed to love you—fully and completely—today and every day for the rest of our lives. Do you remember the jealous time of youth when we believed our love for each other would always flow with heat and fervent passion like a brightly burning flamed Now, of course, we understand that the tension of daily living can put a damper on our passion at times.

Some marriages fall apart when the flame of passion grows dim, but my love for you will remain strong when the flame is burning fiercely and also when it flickers. For, you see, I have chosen to love you—for a lifetime. I rejoice in the commitment I have made to you. It is written upon the pages of my heart.

Dear God,

we come before You this day, reaffirming our love for one another and for You.

Continue to touch our marriage with Your hand of blessing, we pray.

Amen.

Made for Each Other

You formed my inward parts; You covered
me in my mother's womb.

PSALM 139:13 NKJV

My Dear Husband,

You are so very right for me. God made you especially for me—I know it! Each day, I see how perfectly our strengths and weaknesses are being woven together to create a beautiful tapestry. I am so much stronger, so much more courageous, so much more virtuous, so much more fulfilled because you are in my life. Together, we can accomplish anything God asks of us. With His hand of blessing upon our heads, we cannot be defeated.

Do you remember that once we allowed our differences to draw us apart? We think so differently, see issues from differing perspectives, respond differently to the things that happen around us. But we have learned that our differences are the very qualities that give our marriage strength and color and vibrancy. Completing our tapestry will take a lifetime. But as we work together; we will continue to weave a masterpiece.

Dear God,

we thank You wholeheartedly for making us just the way we are.

And we pray that we will both be transformed into all that You would have us become.

Amen.

A man must leave his father and mother
when he marries, so that he can be
perfectly joined to his wife, and the two
shall be one.

EPHESIANS 5:31 TLB

Dear Husband,

I bless you for keeping your promise. Do you remember the day we stood before God and vowed to love and honor each other for as long as we both should lived It was an emotional day, a memorable day, overflowing with roses and promises. It was a day filled with bright expectations and sincere hopes and dreams. It was a day I will always hold close and remember fondly.

Do you recall how I trembled as I looked into your eyes and repeated my vows? I remember the warm security of your embrace and the heat of your kiss. And although time has passed and the roses have faded, my promise to you remains the same. I shall love you as long as I have breath.

Dear God,

help us to reaffirm our
promise to love and
cherish one another
one a daily basis.

Help us to remember
that our marriage
vows were made not
only to each other; but
also to You.

Help us to keep them.

Amen.

The First Time I Saw You

My beloved is white and ruddy, chief
among ten thousand. His head is like the
finest gold; His locks are wavy.

SONG OF SOLOMON 5:10-11 NKJV

My Dear Husband,

You will always be my hero. I remember that unforgettable moment when I first saw you as the person with whom I wanted to spend the rest of my life. In that moment, you became my handsome knight in shining armor—the hero who would slay a fiery dragon to rescue me. And that's when I gave you my heart. I knew we would live happily ever after.

Our marriage has not been the perfect fairy tale we imagined, but you are still my prince. I still feel a glow of excitement and pride when you walk into the room. You will always be my hero, my dragon slayer. I bless the day I placed my hand in yours.

Dear God,

help us to always remember how we felt when our love was new.

And help us to renew our love day by day, in good times and bad, in the storms and in the sunshine.

Amen.

Hidden Places in Our Hearts

Would not God find this out? For He
knows the secrets of the heart.

PSALM 44:21 NASB

My Dear Husband,

I bless you for your hidden depths. Sometimes I watch you when you're unaware that I am looking. And I wonder—what's going on inside that man I love so much? What is he thinking; what is he feeling? For, although we are close, I realize that there are still hidden places in your heart (just as there are in mine)— places where I cannot yet go.

Perhaps those places are uncharted territories for you and, until now, unfathomable to you as well. Perhaps you are only now exploring them yourself. When you are ready, I am anxious to hear of your adventures there. And I long to share some findings of my own, from places within my own heart. In time, with love and trust and patience; perhaps our two hearts can truly become one.

Dear God,

show us the secrets
hidden in the depths
of our own hearts.

And help us to create a
strong foundation of
mutual trust that will
allow us to invite each
other in.

Amen.

When I was a child, I spoke as a child, I
understood as a child, I thought as a child;
but when I became a man, I put away
childish things.

1 CORINTHIANS 13:11 NKJV

My Dear Husband,

I love the little boy in you. I try to imagine you as a small child running barefoot in the grass, playing army soldiers, climbing a big cherry tree, or putting a frog in your pocket. Such thoughts make me smile. I look at your childhood photos and imagine all sorts of things about the charming little boy there. How I wish I had known the child that you were. I think that I would have liked him very much!

I can imagine myself sitting enthralled, listening as you spin your greatest dreams and share your worst fears. I know I would be delighted to find out the little things— like how you felt about asparagus and whether you were in love with your teenaged babysitter. I would have loved you then, in my own childish way, just as I love you now.

Dear God,

I realize how many of the things we experienced in childhood make us who we are today.

Help us to learn more about the children that we were so that we can better appreciate the adults we are now.

Amen.

Let's Grow Old Together

They will still bear fruit in old age, they
will stay fresh and green.
PSALM 92:14 NIV

My Dear Husband,

I bless you for the years we've yet to share. I want
to grow old with you. I want to sit contentedly
upon a wide front porch in a pair of squeaky, old
rockers, visiting happily with you as if we'd only just
met. Or maybe we can travel the countryside together
in a funky, old motor home, seeing the sights for the very
first time. Or perhaps we'll just enjoy our grandchildren
and our great grandchildren.

I want our love to sustain us; I want our interests to
bind us and our commitment to keep us. I want ours to
be the kind of loving relationship that lasts throughout
the years. But I know that kind of love doesn't just happen overnight. It takes time and work, patience and
forgiveness. I know we can get there if we travel hand in
hand, together.

Dear God,

we don't know the number of our days on earth.

But we know that You have put us together.

We ask Your blessing upon our marriage as the years accumulate.

Amen.

I Love Your Eyes

The lamp of the body is the eye. If
therefore your eye is good, your whole
body will be full of light.

MATTHEW 6:22 NKJV

My Dear Husband,

I love what I see in you. Sometimes, when I look deeply into your eyes, it seems that I can glimpse into your soul—a sneak peek into your heart. And how I love what I see there. For your eyes, my love, are like a window to the real you—the you that not everyone else gets to see.

But it saddens me when the drapes are pulled tightly shut, closed against me and everyone else. Although I know I can't force my way inside, how I love it when you open that window for me.

So, please, let me look into your eyes. Let me see what you are thinking, what you are dreaming, what troubles you, and where you have been. Please, don't shut me out.

Dear God,

oh, how I do love
looking into my
husband's eyes.

It makes me feel so
much more in touch
with him, so connected
to his soul.

It is a perfect prelude
to romance.

Amen.

Let's Be Honest

Telling the truth in love, we should grow
up in every way toward Him who is the
Head—Christ.

EPHESIANS 4:15 MLB

My Dear Husband,

I bless you for your honest heart. I know how it can sometimes be painful when we tell the truth. And perhaps that's because we occasionally use honesty as an excuse to vent our frustrations. Although we may think we're "clearing the air," we might actually be creating a great big stink. Yet, I also realize how badly we need an atmosphere of open honesty in our relationship—for we cannot survive without it.

So I want to partner with you. I want to agree that we will speak the truth to one another—but first let's make sure that it's carefully wrapped in a protective layer of love. For it's so much easier to hear the truth when it's cushioned and padded with love.

Dear God,

help us as we pursue
an open and honest
relationship, learning to
speak the truth in love.

Remind us often that
just because
something is true
doesn't mean it must
he said.

Amen.

Why I Cry Sometimes

What happiness there is for you who weep,
for the time will come when you shall
laugh with joy!

LUKE 6:21 TLB

My Dear Husband,

I love it when you understand. I know you realize that men and women are quite different. But when you don't totally understand one of those intricate differences, you sometimes simply shrug them off and move on. What you don't always understand is that sometimes I'm not ready to move on. There are times when I just need a good three-hanky cry (half the time, I don't know why myself).

So don't let my tears make you uncomfortable—they're just part of my emotional makeup. Sometimes they even make things better. Haven't you heard that "crying is good for the soul"? Just be patient with me and I know we can conquer these sensitive areas together.

Dear God,

please help us to tread
softly through those
sensitive areas that
constitute the
differences between us.

Give us the patience
and understanding we
need to support one
another, even when we
don't fully understand.

Amen.

Kindred Spirits

That their hearts may be encouraged,
being knit together in love, and attaining to
all riches of the full assurance of understanding, to the knowledge of the mystery
of God, both of the Father and of Christ.

COLOSSIANS 2:2 NKJV

My Dear Husband,

I bless you for being my other half. I want to be your soul mate—the person you turn to when you need someone to listen—the one you trust with the deepest secrets of your heart. Do you think we can do that for each other? It's a tall order, but with time and God's help, I think we can do it.

I truly believe that when two people come together before God as husband and wife, He opens their hearts to one another in a miraculous way. He makes it possible for them to become kindred spirits. And despite our many differences, I think we fit together beautifully; and our strengths and weaknesses complement one another.

Dear God,

only You are able to
knit our hearts
together and make us
one in Your love.
We pray that You will
teach us to be
willing—and that you
will increase our love
for one another.

Amen.

I forgive You

Be kind toward one another,
tenderhearted, forgiving one another, even
as God has in Christ forgiven you.

EPHESIANS 4:32 MLB

My Dear Husband,

Our forgiveness makes us one. I don't know what it is that makes me want to hold a grudge; but I confess that I do from time to time. It's an unhealthy way to live—and it can be disastrous for a marriage. Please forgive me when I selfishly hold on to an offense and refuse to move on. And thank you for being patient with my shortcomings.

I can't promise you that I'll always be able to forgive quickly, but I do make a commitment to you, even now, that I will ask God to help me turn away from old offenses and let them go, just as He was faithful to let go of mine.

Dear God,

make me quick to
forgive—just as quick
as I am to receive the
forgiveness offered to
me by others; just as
quick as I am to
receive Your
forgiveness for my
own offenses.

Amen.

Even When We Don't Agree

Blessed are the peacemakers, for they will
be called children of God.

MATTHEW 5:9 NRSV

My Dear Husband,

I love that our hearts can agree. Isn't it nice that we don't always have to agree on every single thing? We each have a mind of our own—and I think that makes life vastly more interesting. Or, as one person wisely said, "If we always agreed on everything, then one of us would be unnecessary." What an insight!

So, my love, let's agree to disagree, but let's do it peacefully. Let's welcome those lively discussions, enjoy a good debate, and practice some active listening. But let's take care not to become offensive or defensive, and let's not put each other down when we find ourselves on differing sides of an issue. Let's try hard to see the other point of view. For after all, two heads really are better than one.

Dear God,

teaches us to celebrate our differences and respect our opposing opinions.

Help us to practice love and patience and tolerance, always appreciating the strength we find in varying perspectives.

Amen.

What Are You Thinking?

You know when I sit down and when I rise
up; you discern my thoughts from far
away.

PSALM 139:2 NRSV

My Dear Husband,

I want to know your mind. I've noticed that you seem quiet when you come home some days. You go silently about your business and keep to yourself. Before long, I begin to feel left out and wonder if I've done something wrong. I often worry that something has gone wrong for you during the day or that you are carrying a burden or that you are struggling with a decision I don't know about.

I want you to know that I am here to listen, to offer a warm hug or a shoulder to cry on, if that is what you need. I am also willing to pray quietly for you and give you the space you need to think things through and process your thoughts. Whatever the case, you can count on me. I am on your side always, my love.

Dear God,

help us to respect the
fact that people
sometimes need space
to think and process
their thoughts.
Give us the patience
we need to provide
that for each other.

Amen.

It's Hard to Wait

For I am waiting for you, O Lord my God.
Come and protect me.

PSALM 38:15 TLB

My Dear Husband,

I bless you for your own unique pace. I know I'm pretty impatient at times. Like a child waiting for Christmas, I get all wrought up waiting for things to happen. I want our marriage to be better, our home to be prettier; our lives to be more fulfilling. And although I know my expectations are for positive things, I don't always want to wait for God's timing. I tend to want to anticipate and hurry along. That can make me difficult to live with sometimes.

Please understand, my love. I'm learning to accept that God's timing isn't always my timing. I want to trust Him more completely for what I think I need right now. I pray that soon you will be pleased with the patience God is working in my life.

Dear God,

teach us to appreciate that You have our lives and our days in Your hands.

Remind us that Your timing is always perfect.

Help us to help each other as we wait on You.

Amen.

A Really Good Date

David said to Abigail, "Blessed be the Lord,
the God of Israel, who sent you to meet
me today!"

1 SAMUEL 25:32 NRSV

My Dear Husband,

I love how our love heats up. Do you wonder like I do how to stir up passion and romance in our relationship? Perhaps we should go out on a date periodically—just you and me. No children; no friends. Just the two of us alone together. Whether we walk together on the beach with the wind blowing through our hair or sit in a quiet, candlelit restaurant, let's make it a special time—a time for celebrating our love for each other. It really doesn't matter so much what we do but that we do it. I long to keep alive the wonder of our love and to make sure we kindle it gently with our continuing affections.

I warn you, I plan to look deeply into your eyes, and I may reach for your hand. But I hope you'll be looking into my eyes and reaching for my hand as well. We have a lot of love to share!

Dear God,

give us real romance—
the kind where we
simply lose ourselves in
each other.

And, Lord, help us to
remember to thank
You for planting the
seed of love in our
hearts.

Amen.

Sometimes I Get Moody

As those who have been chosen of God,
holy and beloved, put on a heart of
compassion, kindness, humility, gentleness
and patience.

COLOSSIANS 3:12 NASB

My Dear Husband,

I bless you for your patience. Almost everyone gets moody from time to time—it's just a normal part of everyday living. There's no sense denying it; we both have our moody moments, too.

Let's promise to be patient and understanding when one or the other of us finds that a moody day is under way. Let's decide right here and now that we won't take it personally. We won't make it worse by getting defensive and pouting. We won't try to drag the other to a place of resolution. Let's promise just to love each other through those times and then put them behind us as the sun slips below the horizon.

Dear God,

help us to remember that mood swings are a fact of life.

They have more to do with physiology than with relationships.

Teach us not to personalize them, but to submit our emotions to You and forgive and forget as each day passes.

Amen.

We Need Trust

Like the coolness of snow at harvest time
is a trustworthy messenger to those who
send him; he refreshes the spirit of his
masters.

PROVERBS 25:13 NIV

My Dear Husband,

I trust you with my heart. What is more essential to a healthy friendship than trust? In fact, it is the most basic element of any good relationship. And for our marriage to be all it can possibly be, we must learn to trust each other—implicitly, no matter what, when, or where. But I know that kind of trust doesn't happen overnight. It takes time and working through circumstances and just plain life to build a solid foundation of trust. Yet; we are building it—daily.

Each day that we remain loyal and loving to each other, we place a new stone of trust into our foundation. Let's partner together to build a strong foundation for trust.

Dear God,

we need Your divine
help to build a solid
marriage.

And we need You to
help us to become
dependable and
faithful partners.

We need You to teach
us how to trust each
other.

Amen.

Let's fellowship

If we live in the light, as God is in the light,
we can share fellowship with each other.
Then the blood of Jesus, God's Son,
cleanses us from every sin.

1 JOHN 1:7 NCV

My Dear Husband,

I love seeing you with others. I love spending time with you, and I hope you love spending time with me. But, we both know that we also need other people in our lives. We each need to develop friendships, and if we can enjoy the company of others as a couple, that's even better. Opening our lives to others allows us to give and receive encouragement and insights. And we especially need people in our lives who believe as we do—people who want to love and share and worship God with us.

So, let's make a plan (or maybe just recommit to one) that we will spend time with others. Let's enjoy the fellowship God has graciously provided for us. And let's learn together as a group how to follow after God with whole hearts.

Dear God,

show us where and
when we need to
spend time in
fellowship.

And help us to get in
the habit of going and
sharing—and building
relationships with
others.

Amen.

When the Workday is Done

Let us do our best to go into that place of
rest, too, being careful not to disobey God
. . . thus failing to get in.

HEBREWS 4:11 TLB

My Dear Husband,

I love when we can relax together. Oh, how I look
forward to seeing your face when we come back
together after a long and busy day. And I suppose
I set myself up with all sorts of expectations. Perhaps
I'm discouraged and hoping you'll lift my spirits. Or
maybe I feel happy and want to celebrate. But what I
often forget is that your day may have been the opposite
of mine.

And sometimes we're just out of sync, or maybe we've
both had a rotten day, and we both feel needy and unable
to give. Occasionally emotions rise too quickly to the
surface, and we say things we don't really mean. So, let's
plan for these moments, considering one another and
how we can make more pleasant.

Dear God,

as we look forward to
coming back together
at the end of the day,
help us to seek out
new ways to listen and
encourage each other.

Amen.

Let's Share Our Goals

"I know what I am planning for you," says the Lord. "I have good plans for you, not plans to hurt you. I will give you hope and a good future."

JEREMIAH 29:11 NCV

My Dear Husband,

I bless you for planning ahead. Sometimes I get so caught up in day-to- day responsibilities and events that I neglect to look very far ahead. And to be honest, it worries me to look too far into the future. Besides, aren't we supposed to live one day at a time? But I know you have goals, dear, and we need to discuss them openly.

I have goals, too, but I'm not always sure of the best way to go about achieving them. And I don't always know if they completely align with yours. So, let's keep talking about these things. Let's share our goals, and let's continue planning our lives together with wisdom and patience and discernment.

Dear God,

help us as we sit down together and talk about our future.

Give us the courage to honestly share our goals with each other and plan a strategy for getting there together.

Amen.

> Charm is deceitful and beauty is passing,
> but a woman who fears the Lord, she shall
> be praised.
>
> PROVERBS 31:30 NKJV

My Dear Husband,

I bless you for finding me attractive. I want more than anything else to be beautiful in your eyes, to know that you find me attractive. If you like a certain dress, a particular hairstyle, a special piece of jewelry, or if you like bright colors or soft pastels or pleasant neutrals, then, my love, you can be sure I want to wear them to please you. When I am with you, I am so proud to be your wife. I feel so special when we walk along the street together.

But realistically, bad-hair days happen. And sometimes we all feel as ugly as mud balls. Thank you for letting me know that no matter how I might feel about myself on any given day, I can still walk with confidence, for you see me through the eyes of love.

Dear God,

forgive us when we let
ourselves become
obsessed with our
physical appearance.
Remind us to look at
each other through
loving eyes.

Amen.

Talk to Me

Anxiety in a man's heart weighs it down,
But a good word makes it glad.
PROVERBS 12:25 NASB

My Dear Husband,

I love to hear your voice. Sometimes you can be so quiet. You keep to yourself, and it's as if you have created a bubble of silence around you—or are wearing an invisible sign that says, "Do not disturb." I want to respect your space, your need for quiet and solitude. I know, deep down, that you are not blocking me out so much as blocking yourself in. And I also know that your silence helps you think and sort things out.

But I also need you to talk to me. For silence can be a strange thing sometimes. I can think that your silence means you're unhappy with me—or I can worry that something is wrong in our relationship. And what if you're simply wondering whether your favorite team is going to make it to the Super Bowl? So give me a clue, my love; talk to me. Don't forget how much I like the sound of your voice.

Dear God,

we all have our quiet days.
But remind us to be considerate as we live together in love.

Amen.

The Need to Nurture

> If one member suffers, all suffer together
> with it; if one member is honored, all
> rejoice together with it.
>
> 1 CORINTHIANS 12:26 NRSV

My Dear Husband,

I bless you for being here for me. I like taking care of things, keeping life running smoothly and everyone happy. Perhaps it's just part of my makeup—the need to nurture. And nurturing is good. But sometimes I need to let you nurture me. You may not know this, but you have the innate ability to minister to me and make me feel special like no one else in my life can.

So let's take care of each other. Each day, I will look for ways to ease your stress, encourage your heart, and help you grow stronger in your sense of confidence and well-being. And I will receive with joy the ways in which you nurture me.

Dear God,

show us ways to
nurture and build each
other up.

Teach us to he
sensitive to each
other's needs.

And help us to
appreciate the love and
caring You've placed in
our hearts for each
other.

Amen.

When We Fight

"In your anger do not sin": Do not let the
sun go down while you are still angry, and
do not give the devil a foothold.

EPHESIANS 4:26-27 NIV

My Dear Husband,

I love it when we make up. Most people will agree
that fighting is a natural part of marriage—no
couple agrees on everything all the time (or if
they do, they must be boring!). I don't ever want to fight
with you, but I know there will be times when my human
nature will get the best of me. Before that happens, I
want to make you these promises:

- I will be careful not to call you names.
- I will refuse to dredge up old offenses.
- I won't use phrases like "you always" and "you never."
- I will listen to what you have to say with an open mind.
- I will never criticize you to others.
- I will do my best to never go to bed angry.

Dear God,

teach us to live
peaceably together,
but if we need to clear
the air, help us to do it
in a healthy and
wholesome way.

And may our marriage
be stronger for it.

Amen.

I Need to Be Heard

Don't just pretend that you love others.
Really love them. Hate what is wrong.
Stand on the side of the good.

ROMANS 12:9 NLT

My Dear Husband,

I bless you for listening. Sometimes you must feel that I'm not really listening to you. Perhaps I'm distracted by the TV, involved with projects around the house, or just caught up in my own private thoughts. If this should happen, please don't think that I don't care about you or what you have to say. To me, your words are always important. I look to you for loving feedback.

Just remember that I'm human, and sometimes I forget that nothing is more important than our relationship with each other and with God. I hope that you will gently remind me when I'm set on hyper-speed and not paying attention to the more important things around me.

Dear God,

help us to be sensitive
to each other and
never let the
superficial cares and
responsibilities of
everyday life keep us
from loving and caring
for each other.

Amen.

I Have a Dream

We were like those who dream. Then our
mouth was filled with laughter, and our
tongue with singing . . . "The Lord has
done great things."

PSALM 126:1-2 NKJV

My Dear Husband,

I love to share your dreams. Deep within each of us is a dream—maybe it's from childhood, maybe it's from adolescence, or maybe it is brand-new this very morning It could be silly and frivolous, or serious and intense. Or perhaps it's spiritual and rather difficult to understand. But do you know what my dreams are made of? Do you know what my secret desires might be?

To really know a person, you need to know their dreams, their desires. There's so much more to us than what we see. And love can slowly bring new things to the surface—just like peeling layer after layer off of an onion. So it can be with us.

Dear God,

teach us to dream.
Help us to share our
dreams with each
other.
Show us how to dream
together.

Amen.

Do You Forgive Me?

Bearing with one another, and forgiving
one another, if anyone has a complaint
against another; even as Christ forgave
you, so you also must do.

COLOSSIANS 3:13 NKJV

My Dear Husband,

I bless you for your gracious heart. Okay; I know I'm not perfect, not even close. And, believe me, I know I've hurt you—plenty of times. And for each one of those times, I am truly sorry. Oh how I wish it would never, ever happen again. But unfortunately there doesn't seem to be any pain free formula for love, does there? Yet what is a marriage without it?

But if love is the glue that holds our marriage together, then perhaps forgiveness is the nails. And so, my love, I cherish your forgiveness. I am so grateful that you love me enough to put my offenses behind you and release me from the burden of guilt that always follows when we behave badly.

Dear God,

teach us to practice forgiveness on a daily basis.

Show us how forgiveness is as normal and necessary as the very air we breathe.

Help us to embrace it wholeheartedly and never take it for granted.

Amen.

Let's Light a Candle

My beloved said to me, "Rise up, my love,
my fair one, and come away."

SONG OF SOLOMON 2:10 TLB

My Dear Husband,

I love it when we're together. Let's celebrate romance. Let's plan for a quiet evening at home with fresh flowers, soft music—and let's light some candles. There is something so deeply romantic about the soft, golden glow of candlelight—the way it flickers and casts its delicate light across your skin, the delicious smell of fragrant melting wax, and the warmth of its luminescence as it gently lights the room. The soft scents of musk and rose and jasmine will enhance the expression of our love.

Let's take time to relax and soak in the soft romantic light. Let's talk quietly and intimately, and let's enjoy each other's company. I want to look deeply into your eyes and see the flame of candlelight reflected there—and see the light of love.

Dear God,

thank You for the gift
of romantic love.
Life seems so much
sweeter when the
candlelight is shared by
two.

Amen.

How Can I Help You?

My Dear Husband,

I bless you for inviting my help. Believe it or not, I actually derive real pleasure from helping you. Oh, certainly, I do little daily things for you all the time (things you might even take for granted or barely notice at all). But sometimes I want to help in bigger ways, too—something beyond the ordinary realm. And I love it when you give me the chance to step in.

There might be something you need help with, but you don't think I want to help—or you wonder if I can handle it. But you'll never know if you don't ask. And if it is something I can help with, it will be fun to show you just how clever I am. So, think about it, and give me a chance to prove myself.

Dear God,

give us new ways every day to help each other.

And help us to build confidence in one another by each allowing the other to be creative and try new things.

Amen.

Healing Our Past

The Lord is close to the brokenhearted,
and he saves those whose spirits have been
crushed. People who do what is right may
have many problems, but the Lord will
solve them all.

PSALM 34:18-19 NCV

My Dear Husband,

I love how we can "move on" together. When we entered into our marriage, we both brought along some extra baggage. We were aware of some things and other things we'd forgotten or thought we'd left behind. But as the years pass, old memories resurface, coming out when we least expect them. We soon realize that many wounds from childhood and youth still remain with us. And sometimes they impair our adulthood.

So, let's tell each other about the old hurts that never seem to go completely away. Let's acknowledge them and earnestly pray for each other. And with this new awareness our compassion and understanding for each other will expand—and the healing will begin.

Dear God,

help us recognize and acknowledge the old hurts that have wounded us.

Help us to bring them to You, to pray for each other, and to expect Your healing touch.

Amen.

Celebrating the Years

May the righteous be glad and rejoice
before God; may they be happy and joyful.

PSALM 68:3 NIV

My Dear Husband,

I bless you for the times we've shared. Sometimes the years pass by and we hardly even notice. We get so caught up with the demands of life and our "grown-up" responsibilities that we occasionally forget to celebrate the milestones along the way. We have some achievements worth celebrating. Remember the wonderful feeling we had when we first made our home together? Remember the joy we shared when you were promoted? So, let's not be afraid to greet the oncoming years.

And let's remember to honor the time and energy we've invested into our relationship. Let's rejoice that, through it all, we're still together—still in love and committed to this marriage and our lives together. Let's celebrate the glorious victories of the past, and let's look eagerly forward to the challenges in the future.

Dear God,

we have been through
so much together.
Give us the grace to
rejoice over our
triumphs and celebrate
our successes.

Amen.

Let Me into Your World

It is you, a person like me, my companion
and good friend. We had a good friendship
and walked together to God's Temple.

PSALM 55:13-14 NCV

My Dear Husband,

I love it when you invite me in. Have you ever
considered how we live in two very different
worlds during the course of our day? I must
admit that I sometimes forget that the world you live in
when we're apart is so different from my own.

I'd like to hear more about your world away from me:
what goes on during your workday—what makes you
pull your hair out, what makes you laugh out loud. I wish
I could be a fly on the wall to watch as you go about your
day—to actually see the challenges you face and how you
conquer them. Tell me about them; I'm eager to listen.

Dear God,

there's still so much we don't know about each other, things as simple as our daily routines.

Show us creative ways to share those parts of our lives when we are not together.

Amen.

When Hope Is Deferred

Hope deferred makes the heart sick; but
when dreams come true at last, there is life
and joy.

PROVERBS 13:12 TLB

My Dear Husband,

I bless you for keeping your word. Disappointment is hard to deal with. And when it occurs within our marriage, it takes a heavy toll. So, believe me, my love, I don't like to disappoint you. Sometimes I'm not overly aware that my actions—or my non-actions—are disappointing to you. I try to avoid it whenever possible. And I'm so sorry when I can't, for I realize how discouraging these letdowns can be.

I make this promise today: I will do my best not to make promises to you that I can't keep. And I will work hard, with God's help, to keep my word to you whenever I give it. I want to do everything I can to honor the trust you have placed in me.

Dear God,

teach us to be honorable in our promises to each other.
Show us the importance of keeping our word.

Amen.

A man should leave his father and mother,
and be forever united to his wife. The two
shall become one—no longer two, but one!

MATTHEW 19:5-6 TLB

My Dear Husband,

I love seeing you reach out to others. However, sometimes I think if you and I lived together, all by ourselves, off on a deserted, tropical island somewhere—I think then we could be perfectly happy. Well, at least for a couple of weeks anyway. But there's no getting away from all the other people in our lives; they both bless our lives and complicate them.

Therefore; I want you to know that I will always value your opinion and respect your wishes more than anyone else's. I will put you above my family, my friends, my career, my own needs and desires. I will put you first. In my heart, only God will be higher. I count it an honor to be your wife.

Dear God,

help us to place our relationship above all other earthly ones.

And teach us how to maintain good priorities: putting You first in all things, our marriage second, and everyone else after that.

Amen.

How You Can Help Me

Yes indeed, it is good when you truly obey
our Lord's command, "You must love and
help your neighbors just as much as you
love and take care of yourself."

JAMES 2:8 TLB

My Dear Husband,

I bless you for your strength. I know how I might
sometimes come across as fairly self-sufficient
and capable. I'm always trying to keep things
under control and everyone on track. But underneath
that veneer of togetherness, I am sometimes falling
completely apart inside. I'm grateful that God gave me
someone like you to lean on—someone who is strong
and trustworthy and kind.

When you jump in to help me, suddenly any task
seems doable. I feel immediate relief when your strength
backs my efforts, when your strength doubles mine. It's
fun working with you—and it's true that many hands
make light work. And just think of what fun we can have
once we're done!

Dear God,

teach us how to work together.
Help us to help each other.
Show us some new ways to establish a team spirit when it comes to getting the job done.

Amen.

Sometimes I Don't Know You

May the Lord make your love grow more
and multiply for each other and for all
people so that you will love others as we
love you.

1 THESSALONIANS 3:12 NCV

My Dear Husband,

I love that you're still mysterious. Perhaps one of
life's greatest mysteries is how we could spend
our whole lifetime with one person and still not
really know them. Maybe that's what keeps marriage
alive and fresh and interesting, clear into those olden,
golden years. And I know this is true, for sometimes I
feel like I still don't fully know you.

Sometimes I feel like I don't quite know you when
you do something that seems out of character—or something unexpected or off the wall. But maybe I just need
to expand my definition of who you are. Most of all, I
want to continue to know you better. And it will take
time. But that's okay, because I plan to spend the rest of
my days with you.

Dear God,

we know it isn't necessary to know every single detail about each other right now, so help us to enjoy making fresh discoveries.

Thank You for all the surprises we have in store.

Amen.

What Makes You Tick?

I will be glad and rejoice in your love, for
you saw my affliction and knew the
anguish of my soul.

PSALM 31:7 NIV

My Dear Husband,

I love learning more about you. Thank goodness, we're so vastly different. Have you noticed how one thing totally sets me off but hardly fazes you? Another situation pushes all your buttons and I couldn't care less. Yes, what a blessing that we have such varying temperaments.

Just the same, I sometimes wonder what makes you do the things you do. Is it genetics? A predisposition? Did you have a bad day? A good day? And why do some things tick you off? The reason I want to know is so I can help you. Perhaps I'll see something before you do. Perhaps I can send a gentle warning. Or maybe I can just pray. So, tell me, what makes you tick?

Dear God,

teach us how to be a
blessing to each other,
a leveling influence.
Help us to learn to
depend on each other
to keep our
perspectives well
balanced.

Amen.

I Want to Listen

Be kind to each other, tenderhearted,
forgiving one another, just as God through
Christ has forgiven you.

EPHESIANS 4:32 NLT

My Dear Husband,

I bless you for sharing your heart. I know I appear awfully busy sometimes—I get so caught up in preparations for work or for home or whatever; and I'm sure it could appear that I don't want to be bothered. But you are never a bother. Make no mistake, my love, I always want to have time for you.

But if I'm madly rushing about, I might not notice that you're waiting to be heard. I might need a gentle nudge, a reminder that you're there—that you need my ears. I really do want to listen. Your problems and concerns are mine, and I know how you occasionally need a good sounding board. I'm here for you.

Dear God,

teach us to be good
listeners and to take
time to sit and talk
with each other.

It's easy to get caught
up in the busyness of
life and neglect the
most precious person
in our lives.

Amen.

An Evening with You

How beautiful you are, my love, how
beautiful! Your eyes are soft as doves.
What a lovely, pleasant thing you are, lying
here upon the grass, shaded by the cedar
trees and firs.

SONG OF SOLOMON 1:15-17 TLB

My Dear Husband,

I love just being with you. We don't have to dine at the Ritz, dance until dawn, or even canoe across a moonlit bay. A romantic evening doesn't need to cost a fortune, take hours of time, or require formal wear. Sometimes it's better, and more romantic, just to keep it simple.

Sometimes all I want is a quiet evening with just you and me, alone—together at home. Maybe we can fix a simple meal together (and who knows what can happen in a kitchen?). Or maybe we can take a neighborhood stroll, quietly holding hands as we go. Or perhaps we'll play Scrabble, and I'll let you win for a change. But whatever we do, let's just do it together—the two of us.

Dear God,

remind us to plan quiet times—intimate moments for just the two of us—into the busyness of our lives.

Help us to remember that the most important thing is to be together.

Amen.

Seize the Day!

This is the day the Lord has made; let us
rejoice and be glad in it.

PSALM 118:24 NIV

My Dear Husband,

I love your spontaneity. Sometimes I get so focused on the demanding details of life—ordinary things like laundry and carpools and deadlines—that I completely forget to savor the precious moments of living. And sometimes I need a gentle, but firm, reminder to pause from all my endless activity and to stop and smell the roses—to seize the day.

For only God knows how many earthly days we have to spend together—or how many moments we are allowed where we can embrace and speak those sweet words of love and affection to one another. And when it's all said and done, we'll never regret such pleasant times. So, let's remind each other to enjoy this time we have together—to cherish each new day as a true gift from God.

Dear God,

only You know the span of our lives—but whether they're short or long, each day is unique and special and worthy of celebration.

Teach us to celebrate each one.

Amen.

Let's Take a Walk

The leaves are coming out and the grape
vines are in blossom. How delicious they
smell! Arise, my love, my fair one, and
come away.

SONG OF SOLOMON 2:13 TLB

My Dear Husband,

I love being by your side. There's something so
exquisite about taking a stroll with the one you
love—the warm comforting feeling of holding
hands; the relaxing sense of moving along, unhurried;
the simplicity of enjoying the weather, appreciating the
landscape, and the leisurely rhythm of two pairs of foot-
steps falling into a gentle pace; almost like dancing.

So, let's take a walk together, my love. Let's breathe
deeply of the fresh air and appreciate this rejuvenation
of our spirits, a refreshing of our souls. Whether we
visit quietly as we go or simply listen to the quietness—
drinking in the sounds of birds sweetly singing or the
gentle breeze as it ripples over the land—I know we will
enjoy being together.

Dear God,

simple pleasures always
seem to be the best.
Remind us to take time
to enjoy them
together.

Amen.

Before the dawn comes and the shadows
flee away, come back to me, my love.

SONG OF SOLOMON 2:17 NLT

My Dear Husband,

I love the feel of your hands. I love their confidence; their sureness, their adeptness. I love the assurance I feel when you touch me. I feel so connected to you. Now this might sound a little corny (at first), hut please hear me out. You see, I think we sometimes get so comfortable around each other that we forget to notice the little things—or maybe we've started to take one another just a little for granted. So some evening, when it's all quiet and calm, let's do this simple exercise together.

Let's sit on the floor (cross-legged, if we can), and let's face each other and reach out and touch our palms together, just lightly. And then without speaking, let's just look into each other's face—and I'll try not to giggle. First let's enjoy the sensation of touching palms, then let's close our eyes and "read" each other's faces with our fingertips.

Dear God,

show us creative ways
to open wonderful new
doors in our
relationship, allowing
us to see one another
in a fresh new way.

Amen.

When You Support Me

I will sing of your strength, in the morning
I will sing of your love; for you are my
fortress, my refuge in times of trouble.

PSALM 59:16 NIV

My Dear Husband,

I love how you back me up. Sometimes I really want to try something new, take on afresh challenge, or expand my everyday world just a little. But it can be pretty scary to step out, and I'm not always as confident as I try to appear. The truth is, it almost always seems easier to just do nothing. Perhaps you understand what I'm trying to say.

It's at those times—times when one of us is facing a challenge—that we really need to support one another. When I step out into a new area, it means everything to me to know that you are standing behind me, backing me, cheering me on. Your encouragement means more to me than you can possibly imagine. I want to be there for you in the same way—urging, supporting, cheering.

Dear God,

teach us to be
cheerleaders for each
other, helping us both
to become all that You
have called us to be.

Amen.

Realizing Our Dreams

Help me to do your will, for you are my
God. Lead me in good paths, for your
Spirit is good.

PSALM 143:10 TLB

My Dear Husband,

I love it when our dreams come true. Let's dream
together; my love. Let's talk about our hopes and
aspirations for the future—whether they seem
realistic or not. Let's discuss where we want to be and
how we'd like to get there. Then let's consider ways to
make goals and strategies.

Let's not be afraid to dream big or to dream small.
And let's not be afraid to have our dreams change—for
we are constantly changing.

But most of all, let's be sure to pray for God's guidance
and direction. And let's ask God to enhance and expand
our dreams to match all that He has planned for us. Who
knows, He may choose to give us completely new dreams.
Wouldn't that be exciting!

Dear God,

teach us to dream
Your dreams—and to
dream them together.
Then show us ways of
implementing those
dreams, and help us to
realize them within
our lifetime.

Amen.

Just Tell Me You Love Me

He has brought me to his banquet hall, and
his banner over me is love . . . I am my
beloved's and my beloved is mine.

SONG OF SOLOMON 2:4, 6:3
NASB

My Dear Husband,

I bless you for telling me. Oh, sure, I know they are just words—three little words at that. But they mean so much. I love to hear you whisper them in my ear; those wonderful words, "I love you." They are the life and substance of our relationship. Those words lift me up when I'm down; they heal my spirit when I feel wounded. Those words keep me going when I feel that I can't. Those words are a lifeline for me. I will never tire of hearing you say those three words, "I love you."

I promise to remember to say them to you as well—never to let you go one day without hearing them. They are my pledge of faith to you, renewed day by day. They represent our covenant, the certainty of our union. They are more precious than gold.

Dear God,

help us never to forget
to say those three little
words, "I love you."
They mean so much.

Amen.

Let's Make a Plan

The Lord will guide you always; he will
satisfy your needs in a sun-scorched land
and will strengthen your frame. You will
be like a well-watered garden, like a spring
whose waters never fail.

ISAIAH 58:11 NIV

My Dear Husband,

I bless you taking time. Sometimes it's good to sit down together and make a simple plan—whether it's for a vacation, a weekend away, a home- improvement project, or simply next week's shopping list. Whatever the task, it can be fun and fulfilling to make plans, together with you. And it's rewarding to share ideas and to cooperate with each other. Sure, I know it can try our patience sometimes, but it also teaches us how to give and take—and it improves our listening skills.

It feels so good when we accomplish what we've set out to do. It's exciting to know that we have learned to work together as a team.

Dear God,

show us new and
different ways to plan
and carry out our
plans together.
We know it won't all
go smoothly, but we
believe it will be well
worth the effort.

Amen.

"You must love the Lord your God with all
your heart, all your soul, all your strength,
and all your mind" and, "Love your
neighbor as yourself."

LUKE 10:27 NLT

My Dear Husband,

I love that you think I'm important. There are so many pulls and demands on my life and on yours too. And sometimes the most urgent things appear to be the most important. I often find myself giving those pressing issues my top priority. But if I would only step back and take a couple of deep breaths, I might just realize that they're not so important after all.

If I pause to think about it, I'm often reminded of what's truly important in life. And it's usually quite simple—embarrassingly simple. And, because I love you, I want to remind you, too. First of all, I know it's vitally important for me to love God with my whole heart, to love and cherish you, to love myself, and to love others—in that order. That's the road to true happiness.

Dear God,

thank You for
reminding us to keep
our priorities straight
and simple and to
escape the tyranny of
the urgent.

Amen.

Your Deepest Hurt

For You have delivered my soul from
death, My eyes from tears, And my feet
from falling.

PSALM 116:8 NKJV

My Dear Husband,

I love that you trust me. I know there are still some things about you that you haven't told me yet—or perhaps you've mentioned them in passing but we've not delved too deeply. And it may be that you simply need to tell me all over again. For it's inescapable that we both have old hurts in our lives—some we may have even inflicted upon each other. But our deepest hurts can never heal when left covered up. And they will never heal overnight. The healing process is ongoing and lifelong.

So, if you need to talk about an old hurt, my love, I invite you to come to me. I want to hear (even if I've heard it before). And then let's agree to pray together— let's pray that God will continue the healing work that He's begun in both our lives.

Dear God,

when one of us hurts,
the other does as well.
Make us ever ready to
listen and to submit
our hurts to You so
that we both might be
healed and whole.

Amen.

Make your ear attentive to wisdom, incline
your heart to understanding.

PROVERBS 2:2 NASB

My Dear Husband,

Your intelligence is valuable to me. I know our tastes differ in some areas, but I think it's possible to find some common ground in literature—if we're willing to try, that is, and willing to compromise a little. So, let's go together and select a good book, one that we'll both want to read and enjoy. It can be a novel, a biography, a how-to, or whatever—as long as we both agree. And then let's read the book together.

Perhaps we could take turns reading aloud to each other at bedtime. Or maybe we could each read the same chapter, separately, and discuss it later. Maybe we should read the entire book and then talk about it, discussing what we liked and what we didn't. What do you think?

Dear God,

it's important to bring our minds together so that we can experience something new and grow as individuals and as a couple.

Help us to find a book to read together that will bless us both.

Amen.

Forgive and Try to Forget

When you stand praying, if you hold
anything against anyone, forgive him, so
that your Father in heaven may forgive you
your sins.

MARK 11:25 NIV

My Dear Husband,

I bless you for forgetting my past mistakes. Probably the hardest part of forgiving each other is trying to blot out memories of past hurts. And although we hear people say, "forgive and forget," we both know it's not easy. Short of amnesia or a lobotomy, I'm not sure it's even possible. But I hope that over time we can put some memories to rest and move forward.

Let's try to put old things behind us as we forgive each other. And let's make it our earnest goal not to dredge up any old hurts, but instead let's focus our energy on healing and wholeness and love. For it seems that love, above all else, is able to clean the slate. So, let's follow love's lead—let's forgive and, in time, forget.

Dear God,

we know how vital
forgiveness is to our
marriage.
It's never easy to
forget a past offense.
Please send Your love
to wash away the hurt.

Amen.

What Are Your Dreams?

Every day and all night long their counsel
will lead you and save you from harm;
when you wake up in the morning, let their
instructions guide you into the new day.

PROVERBS 6:22 TLB

My Dear Husband,

Your dreams are important to me. Do you have some secret dreams hidden away in your heart? Perhaps they've been sleeping there since childhood and might even seem silly to you now. Or maybe they're recent dreams, but they seem too impossible or unlikely to be shared with someone else, or maybe even too wild and ridiculous to mention out loud.

But you can tell me, my love. Even if they're strange things, like wanting to join the circus, or leap out of highflying airplanes, or play drums in a rock 'n' roll band, I still want to hear all about them. And I promise to try to be a good listener. So, trust me and consider sharing your aspirations. Please tell me your dreams.

Dear God,

continue to teach us
how important trust is
to our marriage.
Give us the courage to
share our dreams with
You and with each
other.

Amen.

Your Strong Hands

We are His workmanship, created in Christ
Jesus for good works, which God prepared
beforehand that we should walk in them.

EPHESIANS 2:10 NKJV

My Dear Husband,

I bless you for your touch. I love your hands. I love their strength and power; I love their tender gentleness. I love the feel of your fingers wrapping themselves securely around my own. I love the warm squeezes you give to support and encourage me during a difficult time. I love the kindness I see when your hands reach out to help someone. And I love to see your hands picking up a small child. I just love your hands.

I love when your fingers gently massage the tight muscles in the back of my neck. How I love the way you affectionately tousle my hair. And I love the feel of your index finger slowly tracing the curve of my cheek. Your, hands are a symbol of your love for me, and oh, how I treasure them.

Dear God,

thank You for the wonderful connection that we can make through touch.

It is a gift from You.

Thank You for the gentleness and strength that touch conveys.

Amen.

I Know What You're Thinking

When my anxious thoughts multiply
within me, Your consolations delight my
soul.

PSALM 94:19 NASB

My Dear Husband,

Your thoughts intrigue me. Now, don't worry, it doesn't happen all the time. And honestly, I don't claim to be clairvoyant or some kind of mystical mind reader. But sometimes, my love, I think I know what you're thinking. And occasionally I hear your words before they touch your lips. Maybe it's because we've been together awhile or we're just in sync.

It's not a bad thing, not at all. It's probably just the inevitable reward of two people loving each other like we do. And it brings me joy to know what's on your mind. So, don't take offense the next time I say, "I knew you were going to say that." But rejoice that our hearts and minds are becoming one.

Dear God,

continue to knit our
lives together; help our
hearts and minds to
unite in understanding.

It's Your divine will
that two become one
in Your love.

Amen.

Home Matters

Everyone who hears these words of mine
and puts them into practice is like a wise
man who built his house on the rock.

MATTHEW 7:24 NIV

My Dear Husband,

I bless you for our home. Some say that a house is more important to a woman because it's more of a reflection on her than on her husband. But I've come to believe that it's a more true reflection of us—a visual aid that spotlights the condition of our relationship. When our marriage functions well, I think our home runs more smoothly. And if the home front is lagging, perhaps we need to invest more time in our relationship.

I long to have a warm and open home where we both feel at ease and comfortable, but I can't do it without you. So, take a look around our home. Is it all that it could be—or is there room for improvement? Let's start with what really matters—us.

Dear God,

give us the grace to partner together to make our home a true reflection of our marriage.

Help us to appreciate elements like warmth, beauty, and comfort, and make our hearts feel at home.

Amen.

Tell Me Where It Hurts

Put on the full armor of God so that you can fight against the devil's evil tricks. Our fight is not against people on earth but . . . against the spiritual powers of evil in the heavenly world.

EPHESIANS 6:11-12 NCV

My Dear Husband,

I am here to help. Some days you come home from work looking like the walking wounded. Your steps are heavy and leaden; your shoulders sag as if you're carrying half the world; and your brow is creased. And I grow concerned and want to help, but I also realize that you might need some quiet time to decompress

I hope when you're ready, you'll feel free to come and tell me where it hurts. I want you to show me where you've been injured, and together we can soothe and bandage your wounds. And hopefully we can get you whole and ready to return to the battlefield.

Dear God,

teach us to help and
encourage each other
when we're hurt.

Help us to remember
that we need to wear
Your armor wherever
we go so that You can
protect us.

Amen.

Worshipping Together

Oh come, let us worship and bow down;
Let us kneel before the Lord our Maker.
For He is our God, And we are the people
of His pasture, And the sheep of His hand.

PSALM 95:6-7 NKJV

My Dear Husband,

I love when we both look to God. Such amazing things happen when I stand next to you and we worship Him. Whether we're praying together amidst the congregation, or singing hymns with the choir, or silently worshiping in the pew—something totally unexpected and incredible takes place inside my heart. For whenever we worship God together, with honest and open spirits, I feel closer to you than ever.

So, let's take advantage of these opportunities to worship with each other. Let's make sure we take time to attend services and gather together with other believers. And let's remind ourselves that one day we will bow before the throne of God and worship at His feet—still standing side by side.

Dear God,

teach us to come
together before You—
to honor and worship
and praise You.

Unite our hearts as
never before.

Amen.

Looking Ahead

A house is built by wisdom and becomes
strong through good sense. Through
knowledge its rooms are filled with all
sorts of precious riches and valuables.

PROVERBS 24:3-4 NLT

My Dear Husband,

I love looking forward with you. Building our marriage is a lot like building a house. If we take the time and invest the energy, it should protect and sustain us through the oncoming years. And when I consider the future, I smile as I imagine us growing older together, getting closer; our relationship deepening with time. I think a love like ours can only improve with age.

Like a beautifully built older home, with mature landscaping and a beautiful patina to the woodwork, I imagine our marriage growing more and more lovely with each passing year. But like an older home, I know we'll need to continue doing careful maintenance——-for neglect can lead to ruin. But our reward will be a wonderful haven of love.

122

Dear God,

teach us to recognize
the everyday increasing
value of our marriage.

Show us how to care
for it as if it were a
priceless investment—
which, in fact, it is.

Amen.

Are You Really from Mars?

Take a look at the hippopotamus! I made
him, too, just as I made you!

JOB 40:15 TLB

My Dear Husband,

I bless you for being different. There's a rumor
going around that you're from Mars and I'm
from Venus, but I happen to believe we're both
the byproducts of God's amazing creativity combined
with His wonderful sense of humor. Although, to be
honest, sometimes it can seem as if we actually came
from two entirely different worlds.

Let's learn to treat our differences with the same
dignity we would show a foreign guest. Instead of con-
forming a visitor to our traditions and culture, we would
more likely express interest and respect for his ways and
try to learn from him. So let's appreciate our differing
perspectives and unique backgrounds—and let's learn
from each other. Your masculinity and my femininity
were custom made by God.

Dear God,

forgive us for the
times we have failed to
appreciate the
differences You've
placed within us.

Help us to see each
other with new eyes.

Amen.

Mixed Memories

Who sees anything different in you? What do you have that you did not receive? And if you received it, why do you boast as if it were not a gift?

1 CORINTHIANS 4:7 NRSV

My Dear Husband,

I bless you for how you see things. Do you remember what I was wearing when we first met? Do you remember the color? Do you recall what you were wearing? Well, we don't always remember things in the same way, do we?

Perhaps it's because our memories latch on to different things, and neither one of us is completely right or completely wrong. Consider two people describing the same house (one from inside and one from outside). One says the house is blue and one says the house is white—and though their opinions differ, they're both right. I think we could learn a lot by comparing notes.

Dear God,

help us not only to respect our different perspectives, but to enjoy the varied interest we both bring to this marriage.

Thank You for our uniqueness.

Amen.

Two Hearts Becoming One

A man should leave his father and mother,
and be forever united to his wife. The two
shall become one—no longer two, but one!

MATTHEW 19:5-6 TLB

My Dear Husband,

I love that we're united. When we made our wedding vows, I imagined that our hearts became instantly united just by the mere speaking of those powerful words. But now, as time has passed, I realize that this marriage union is a daily and continuing process. And no matter how hard we try, that kind of "oneness" just doesn't happen overnight.

But I truly want my heart to be united with yours—I long for our two hearts to become one. I believe that this can only happen when we surrender our hearts to God, totally entrust our marriage to Him, and allow Him to do the uniting. For what God joins together, no human being can ever pull apart.

Dear God,

we agree to put our marriage completely in Your capable hands.

Give us direction and guidance, and bind our hearts together in Your love.

Amen.

On Those Special Days

Shout joyfully to the Lord, all the earth;
Break forth and sing for joy and sing
praises.

PSALM 98:4 NASB

My Dear Husband,

Thank you for remembering. Throughout the year, holidays and birthdays and various celebrations occur. And I've come to realize that due to our unique backgrounds and upbringings, we view these momentous occasions differently. We both bring a differing set of expectations and customs to our marriage. I admit that I sometimes forget this important fact. Whether we open presents on Christmas Eve or Christmas morning, for example, isn't as important as that we celebrate together and create new customs. We can have the best of both worlds!

Forgive me if I've frustrated and even disappointed you when these special days have not gone the way you expected them to. Let's agree to discuss and plan these times well in advance. And let's both be willing to compromise as we build our own new traditions.

Dear God,

we lay all our hopes
and expectations
before You.

Help us to plan
together to make the
most of those special
times and to draw
closer to You and to
each other as a result.

Amen.

Sometimes I Watch You

Like an apple tree among the trees of the forest, So is my beloved among the young men. In his shade I took great delight and sat down, And his fruit was sweet to my taste.

SONG OF SOLOMON 2:3 NASB

My Dear Husband,

I love what I see in you. I like to watch you when you're interacting with someone else or intently focusing on a favorite hobby or sometimes simply sleeping. I like to study your face—the little lines that are beginning to appear around your eyes, the shape of your nose, the curve of your earlobe, the jut of your chin.

But even more than that, I like to watch your facial expressions—the way your brow slightly furrows with concern when you see a friend in some sort of difficulty. Or the way you grow thoughtful when someone asks a provoking question. Or how the corners of your mouth curl up just before you laugh.

Dear God,

thank You for the
little things that we
enjoy so much about
each other.

Thank You for the
love that makes those
things so special.

Amen.

Your love has given me great joy and
encouragement, because you, brother, have
refreshed the hearts of the saints.

PHILEMON 7 NIV

My Dear Husband,

I bless you for your help. Life's stresses and demands can take their toll on me. Sometimes I
just get plain tired and fatigued. Like an engine
running on empty, I start to slow down and lag behind,
and sometimes I don't even realize how it all happened
or even why.

It's times like these when I really need you. I need
your patience and your understanding and your gentle
encouragement. Perhaps I even need you to encourage
me to slow down and rest or to point out how I've been
neglecting myself in my frenzy to keep on going. The
truth is, I often do put my needs after everyone else's—
and a loving reminder from you can prevent me from
getting weary.

Dear God,

help us to he sensitive to the weariness and fatigue that comes as a result of giving ourselves to those we love.

Help us to watch over each other with care and to gently remind each other to rest.

Amen.

Here's to You

He who loves a pure heart and whose
speech is gracious will have the king for his
friend.

PROVERBS 22:11 NIV

My Dear Husband,

I love you just the way you are. I know sometimes you must think that all I see are your flaws. But that's not really how I see you—not truly. I hope you'll forgive me for being critical or negative at times.

For the truth is, I see absolutely wonderful things in you—the same things that first attracted me to you. But perhaps I take them for granted. If I were to make a two-column list of your traits, with the positives on one side and the negatives on the other, the good would far outweigh the bad. In fact, your positives are so overwhelming that it's a little silly to focus so much on the negatives. So, let me say how much I appreciate you. I'm so glad that you're mine and I'm yours. And, I want you to know with certainty that I think you're the best.

Dear God,

forgive us when we are critical and negative with each other.

Help us to point out the good things, the wonderful things we love about each other.

Amen.

You Make Me Complete

In the same way, we are many, but in
Christ we are all one body. Each one is a
part of that body, and each part belongs
to all the other parts.

ROMANS 12:5 NCV

My Dear Husband,

I love what I learn from you. Okay, it's not as if I don't consider myself a whole and entire person —because I know that I am. But on the other hand, I believe that being married to you somehow makes me more complete. It's hard to understand or even explain how this little miracle actually works. I think it must be another one of God's great mysteries. But just the same, I'm so thankful for it.

For you've stretched me in all kinds of areas—the way nothing else ever could. And as I live and learn in our relationship, I honestly believe I become a bigger person—more loving, forgiving, and kind. And I hope I do the same for you.

Dear God,

thank You for putting
us together, for seeing
that we would be good
for each other.

We know we are both
better people because
we are together, and
we appreciate it.

Amen.

The Way We Were

I remember the days of old; I meditate on
all Your doings; I muse on the work of
Your hands.

PSALM 143:5 NASB

My Dear Husband,

I love our old memories. It's fun to look back over old photos of ourselves and suddenly realize how much we've changed over the years. When we take time to remember just where we've been, we can better appreciate how far we've come in our relationship, in our love for each other. But it's also a good time to consider whether we've left anything valuable behind.

How did we view each other back then? Were we superficial? Idealistic? Unrealistic? Did we dream big dreams together? Have we forgotten some? And how did we see the world we lived in? Were we simplistic? Overwhelmed? Hopeful? Let's remember the way we were—and how we've become who we are.

Dear God,

remind us that
considering the past
often helps us to
better understand the
present and better plan
for the future.

Help us to look back
together with curiosity
and honesty.

Amen.

Let's Turn Down the Lights

My beloved is like a gazelle or a young
stag. Look, there he stands behind our wall,
gazing in at the windows, looking through
the lattice.

SONG OF SOLOMON 2:9 NRSV

My Dear Husband,

I bless you for our romance. Something magical
happens when you turn the lights down low—
especially when there's a soft glow of candlelight
combined with sweet tones of music. Haven't you noticed
how a romantic hush can settle over a dimly lit room,
how the shadows can magically obscure the distractions
and simply push them far away from us?

Suddenly it's just you and me—alone together—in
our undisturbed little world. You become my focus and
I become yours. And we can take the time to sit together;
enjoying quiet and intimate conversation, sweet nuances,
the pleasure of familiarity, the expectation of things to
come. So, turn down the lights, my love.

Dear God,

help us never to minimize the need for romance in our relationship.
It reminds us that we need each other and that we enjoy the pleasure of being together.

Amen.

I'm Here for You

Though one might prevail against another,
two will withstand one. A threefold cord is
not quickly broken.

ECCLESIASTES 4:12 NRSV

My Dear Husband,

I love cheering you on. I think there's a tiny part of every little girl that wants to become a cheerleader. And, who knows, maybe that's the way God made us—so that one day we could stand up and cheer for our man, bolstering him with our support and encouragement. That's the way I want to cheer you on. I want to clap my hands and say, "Go, fight, win!" And you know what? You will!

I'm here for you, my love. I'm standing behind you (and beside you). I hope and believe the very best for you and your life. Your success is my success (and mine, yours). By the same token, your disappointment is also mine. So whatever happens, for better or for worse, I am here for you.

Dear God,

we thank You for
placing us together.
This life would be so
lonely if we had to
face it alone.

What a powerfully
victorious team the
three of us can be.

Amen.

Sometimes I Get Busy

It will be a sign between me and the
Israelites forever, for in six days the Lord
made the heavens and the earth, and on
the seventh day he abstained from work
and rested.

EXODUS 31:17 NIV

My Dear Husband,

I bless you for your patient reminders. Life occasionally gets pretty hectic around here, and sometimes I literally can't remember if I'm coming or going. It often seems I've got a dozen things to take care of—all at once—and that's before breakfast! When I get busy and distracted with the demanding details of life; I sometimes forget to communicate very carefully, or thoughtfully, and I can become impatient. And in my heart, I'm sorry.

You can help me during these stressful times by gently reminding me to slow down and keep my priorities in order. I welcome your tender correction, for it is my desire to be the best wife I can be to you and to be a blessing to your life.

Dear God,

we all get busy sometimes and it's difficult to say no.

Help us to gently remind each other to slow down when the busyness gets too great.

Amen.

Please forgive Me

Bear with each other and forgive whatever
grievances you may have against one
another. Forgive as the Lord forgave you.

COLOSSIANS 3:13 NIV

My Dear Husband,

I bless you for your forgiving heart. It's painfully true—I do actually blow it from time to time. And I'm sure there have been plenty of times when I haven't even said I was sorry—not to mention the times when I haven't paused to ask you for your forgiveness. Oh, I could try to make excuses now, but they would probably just boil down to things like selfishness or pride—so I won't bother.

Instead, I want to say I'm truly sorry for the many times I've hurt you and haven't apologized. And I'm sorry that I haven't always asked you to forgive me. But I thank you for the times you have forgiven me anyway. Your forgiveness means more to me than I can even say. It's like a stream of fresh flowing water quenching a thirsty soul.

Dear God,

a marriage without grace and forgiveness will quickly die.

Thank You for reminding us to forgive each other.

Amen.

When I Think of You

> I am sending him to you for the express purpose that you may know about our circumstances and that he may encourage your hearts.
>
> COLOSSIANS 4:8 NIV

My Dear Husband,

Just the thought of you warms me. Sometimes in the midst of a trying situation, or if it seems the whole world has turned against me, you come to mind. And when I think of you, I am comforted and encouraged. Maybe it's because I can imagine your strong arms around me or I can envision your smile or I can hear you whisper sweet words of love and kindness into my ear.

Somehow, just thinking of you brings a quiet sense of peace and joy to my heart. And then I instantly grow thankful that you and I will come back together at the end of the day. I know how you'll listen to my tales of woe and how you'll console me, and maybe we'll laugh about the whole silly thing together. Thank you for loving me.

Dear God,

the world is a warmer,
friendlier place
because we have each
other.
Thank You for giving
us the ability to
comfort one another.

Amen.

I Need Your Love

Now faith, hope, love, abide these three;
but the greatest of these is love.

1 CORINTHIANS 13:13 NASB

My Dear Husband,

I bless you for your tender love. I'm always declaring one kind of need or another. How often I need your help with mundane; but necessary, things like taking out the trash, getting the car checked, or cleaning the gutters. And then sometimes I simply need you to hold my hand, to stroke my hair, or to tell me everything's going to be okay.

But I don't usually admit how much I need your love. I think there's something inside us that doesn't like to acknowledge such deeply felt needs. Maybe we're afraid of what might happen if those needs were denied. But the fact is, I need your love—desperately. Your love means everything to me. Without it, I would be nothing.

Dear God,

love is the lifeblood of
our marriage.
We need Your love and
the love we bring to
each other.
Remind us to always
give our love freely.

Amen.

Accepting My Friends

Do not forsake your own friend or your
father's friend, And do not go to your
brother's house in the day of your
calamity; Better is a neighbor who is near
than a brother far away.

PROVERBS 27:10 NASB

My Dear Husband,

Thank you for being gracious. Okay, let's be honest and admit it—my friends aren't always your friends. Nor are yours mine. And although it can sometimes be a bone of contention, I think we can get past it, if we try. Because the fact is, just as you and I are different (and we're learning to accept and appreciate those differences), so our friends are different too.

I make this commitment to you now: I will try to see the good in each of your friends. I will work hard to understand why each of these friends is so important to you, what each one brings to your life. I hope you will do the same for me. I know we will be happier when we see the good in every person who is a part of our lives.

Dear God,

help us not to be
jealous or resent the
friends You put in each
of our lives.

Give us an honest
appreciation for them.

Remind us that You
love each person.

Amen.

A friendly face

A cheerful look brings joy to the heart;
good news makes for good health.

PROVERBS 15:30 NLT

My Dear Husband,

I love to see your smile. You know how you can be having one of those really crummy days where no matter how hard you try, nothing ever goes right, and it starts to feel as if that day will never end? So often when that happens to me, out of the blue, you call me just to say, "I love you." Or, even better, you show up. And suddenly, there you are just smiling at me—and somehow when I see your friendly, grinning face, it assures me that I can make it.

I also love it when we go to a place full of people I don't even know and who don't seem eager to know me, and I spot your face in the crowd. Oh, how I appreciate that, especially when you look right into my eyes and smile. Your love is my most cherished possession.

Dear God,

a smiling and friendly face is like a healthy tonic.

It refreshes and invigorates the soul.

Help us always to appreciate the gift You have given us as we look into each other's welcoming eyes.

Amen.

You're My Best Friend

There are "friends" who pretend to
befriends, but there is a friend who sticks
closer than a brother.

PROVERBS 18:24 TLB

My Dear Husband,

I bless you for your friendship. It's no secret that strong friendships fortify the best of marriages. And when I see a couple who enjoys the same kinds of activities and each other's company, I suspect they have a relationship destined to go the distance. And that's what I desire for us. I want to be your very best friend, and I want you to be mine.

I know it takes time and commitment to be best friends, but I believe it's worth it. I want to be that sort of dependable friend to you. So, let's agree to set our friendship above all others. Let's come together with honest and caring hearts. Let's pursue common interests and spend plenty of quality time together.

Dear God,

please help us build a
lasting friendship.
Teach us about
commitment and love,
show us ways to
develop similar
interests, and join our
hearts as friends.

Amen.

What Does It Matter?

As God's chosen ones, holy and beloved,
clothe yourselves with compassion,
kindness, humility, meekness, and patience.

COLOSSIANS 3:12 NRSV

My Dear Husband,

Thanks for knowing what's important. Why should we bother to take time to be alone? Does it really matter? And what difference does it make if we forget to kiss goodbye when we part? Or if we don't say "goodnight"? What does it matter if we forget to say, "I love you"? Aren't these things we can take for granted?

Of course not. Our love does matter. Our daily reminders help us keep the importance of our relationship in the forefront of our lives. And I promise you I will always treasure your love for me and nurture my love for you. How glad we will be that we took time to do these things so that our love would flourish and grow. Let's work hard to keep our love alive.

Dear God,

don't let us tolerate apathy and passivity in our marriage.

Remind us never to take our love or marriage for granted.

We commit ourselves to honor it as a living gift from You.

Amen.

Fanning the Flame

Let him kiss me with the kisses of his
mouth— For your love is better than wine.

SONG OF SOLOMON 1:2 NKJV

My Dear Husband,

I bless you for the heat of your love. What do you do when passion's embers burn low? Do you know how to fan the flame of romance back into a hotly burning fire? Which reminds me how someone once said that true romance begins in the kitchen (of course, if you can't take the heat, you better stay out). So, my love; let's be certain to ignite romance in every room by doing those things that keep love burning brightly.

Don't you agree that true romance begins with a kind and caring attitude? It can start with gentleness and helping hands. Maybe it's a look of appreciation, a thoughtful word, or a tender touch. And like some recipes, it must slowly simmer before coming to a boil. So let's gently fan the flame and see what we can cook up.

Dear God,

teach us how to be
kind and good to one
another, always
remembering that love
is strongest when it is
given away.

Amen.

I Believe in You

Many people claim to be loyal, but it is
hard to find a trustworthy person. The
good people who live honest lives will be a
blessing to their children.

PROVERBS 20:6-7 NCV

My Dear Husband,

I bless your success. I know you're not perfect—
just as you know that I'm not. I probably know
more about your mistakes than anyone else on
earth. Yet, I surely love you more than any other person
does except God! Why?

It's because I believe in you. I believe that you're a
truly wonderful person. I believe that you will succeed
at whatever you put your mind to. I believe in your
diligence, your strength, your intelligence, your heart,
and much more. And I will always believe in you, my
love. You are destined for great things.

Dear God,

teach us to trust You more by believing in each other.

And though this kind of trust can make us feel vulnerable, we know we can rely on You to sustain us through all things.

Amen.

Let's Make Some Time

To everything there is a season, a time for
every purpose under heaven.

ECCLESIASTES 3:1 NKJV

My Dear Husband,

Thanks for valuing our time together. How often do we say we'll do this or that or that we'll go here or there "when we have the time"? But time seems to pass so quickly. Before we realize it, the time is gone and we haven't done any of the things we meant to do. So instead of waiting until we have the time—let's decide right here and now to make the time, and then let's take the time to do those things we've talked about.

Let's sit down with our calendars and make a plan together. Let's block out time that belongs only to us—to our relationship—to our marriage. Whether it's a few days away, a weekly date night, or a meeting for lunch— let's get it in writing and commit to do it. Our love is worth making time for.

Dear God,

only You know how
many days we have
together in this life.

Help us to be wise,
plan ahead, make the
time we need, and then
take it and enjoy it.

Amen.

Totally Devoted

Greater love has no one than this, that one
lay down his life for his friends.

JOHN 15:13 NASB

My Dear Husband,

My love for you is total. Remember the romantic story of Romeo and Juliet—how they loved each other so completely that they were willing to die for each other? Okay, I admit they were both very young and, after all, only fictional—but wouldn't it be great to share that kind of love and devotion? I want to be so totally devoted to you that I would be willing to lay down my life for you, if necessary—and know that you would do the same for me.

I long for that incredible depth of passion and commitment in our relationship. And I pray that as our love deepens, our devotion to each other will grow as well. With God's help, I want to learn to love you unselfishly and completely.

Dear God,

we realize that perfect
devotion can only
come from You.

Teach us to love each
other so fully that we
would each gladly lay
down ourselves and
put the other person
first.

Amen.

Can you fathom the mysteries of God? Can
you probe the limits of the Almighty?
They are higher than the heavens—what
can you do? They are deeper than the
depths of the grave—what can you know?

JOB 11:7-8 NIV

My Dear Husband,

I love that we've more to learn. Do you think you know everything about me? Well, I've got good news. There are still some things you don't know, things we've never yet discussed, areas still waiting to be explored. And by the same token, I'm sure there are some places in you where I've never been.

These are places that will take a lifetime to uncover. Things that should be revealed slowly, with the greatest amount of trust. The more I learn about you, the more I love you. But isn't that the wonderful mystery of our relationship—that even after all the time we've been together, we still have some unexplored territory to discover?

Dear God,

thank You for making
us infinitely interesting
to each other.
It will take a lifetime
to reveal all the
mysteries of who we
are to one another.
How delightful that
will be.

Amen.

You will . . . be happy and dance merrily
with timbrels.

JEREMIAH 31:4 TLB

My Dear Husband,

I love it when we celebrate our love. Let's listen to some really good music—something we both like—something that makes us want to get onto our feet and move to its rhythm. It can be fast and energetic; or it can be slow and soulful. But let's allow the music to flow right through us, and then let's cast our inhibitions aside, and let's dance. You can be my Fred, and I will be your Ginger. You lead so well in the rest of our lives, and I want to follow your lead on the dance floor as well.

Before the night is over, let's make sure we dance slowly. I want to feel the warmth of your body and the security of your arms around me as we sway gently, moving together. For our souls seem to meld as our feet move us across the floor. Come on, baby, let's dance.

Dear God,

thank You for the fun
of spending time
together and with You.
For laughter and
happy times, for
warmth and security,
for energy and soul, we
thank You.

Amen.

I consider the days of old, and remember
the years of long ago. I commune with my
heart in the night; I meditate and search
my spirit.

PSALM 77:5-6 NRSV

My Dear Husband,

I love my memories of us. Sometimes we need to take a trip down memory lane. We need to replay our history together—to, in essence, celebrate us and how far we've come. For we are like a beautiful story, even as it's being told. And it's pleasant to hear the words, turn the pages, remember the beginning, and even guess at the ending.

How well I remember the first time I saw your face. That moment will always be crystallized in my mind. Do you recall the first time you met me? What did you think? What did you say? What did you want to say? And how about the first time we actually had a conversation? Do you remember what we talked about? Do you recall our first date and where we went, what we did? And how about that first kiss? What were you thinking then?

Dear God,

help us to remember
the special moments
that we've shared
together.
And thank You for
showing us how far
we've come.

Amen.

Total Truth

Speaking the truth in love, we will in all
things grow up into him who is the Head,
that is, Christ.

EPHESIANS 4:15 NIV

My Dear Husband,

I love your honesty with me. Any healthy relationship has a solid foundation of openness and honesty beneath it. And that's what I long for with us. I want you to always feel you can be completely candid with me; even if it's not totally comfortable. For how can we grow and change in our relationship if we shy away from the truth? And doesn't the truth, after all, set us free?

But let's remember not to use honesty as an excuse to bluntly wound each other. Let's keep in mind that love must always accompany truth—that truth without love can be painful. And let's also agree to quietly listen to the truth, even when it hurts—then we can allow time to process it, believing that the end results are well worth it.

Dear God,

we need honesty in our relationship.

Show us how to speak the truth in love, teach us to react with wisdom and dignity, and help us to grow closer together.

Amen.

When We Get Angry

My beloved brethren, let every man be
swift to hear, slow to speak, slow to wrath.

JAMES 1:19 KJV

My Dear Husband,

I bless you for your self-control. I know that everyone gets angry sometimes. It's simply a normal part of life, and sometimes a little loud venting is a good way to clear the air and move on. It can even be a good way to draw our attention to a real problem that needs to be addressed. But there are also those times when anger can hurt us and those around us—and that's when we need to reevaluate this potentially dangerous emotion.

For like a bubbling pot with too much heat beneath it, anger can boil over and scald those who stand too close. But kind and gentle words can cool a very hot situation—a loving spirit can graciously turn down the flame. If we work together and ask God for help, we can both learn to manage and control our anger.

Dear God,

uncontrolled anger
hurts our marriage.
Help us to avoid this
trap and strive to live
in peace.

Amen.

When We Pray Together

All things for which you pray and ask,
believe that you have received them, and
they will be granted you.

MARK 11:24 NASB

My Dear Husband,

I love that our hearts can agree in prayer. It's certainly not the easiest thing to do. And it seems there are always a dozen reasons why we can't and don't—it's too late, too early, or we're too busy, too tired. For some reason, it's just easier not to pray together. But here's the amazing thing: When we actually do sit down and really pray together, something incredible happens in our hearts and souls. It seems we are bound together in power and in strength; our spirits unite and we become one.

Just the same, it can be difficult for me to ask you to pray. For some reason I tend to wait, hoping you will lead the way. Together, let's discover the best ways we can join our hearts in prayer. And then, no excuses, let's just do it.

Dear God,

help us come together
to decide how we can
become better prayer
partners, whether with
a prayer list or in silent
prayer.

Show us the way.

Amen.

I'm Lost Without You

He saves them from death and spares their
lives in times of hunger. So our hope is in
the Lord. He is our help, our shield to
protect us.

PSALM 33:19-20 NCV

My Dear Husband,

I love that you're my true north. Of course, I like you to think I'm a fairly independent person—able to confidently handle and conquer most parts of my day with little or no help. But the truth is, if you're away from home for just a day or two, I begin to feel rather lost without you. I notice your absence during all my waking moments. But to be honest, I'm relieved to feel this way.

For when I'm missing you like that, I realize how connected our lives truly are. I become acutely aware of how important you are to me and how empty my life would be without you in it. I need you sleeping beside me. I need your smile to start my day. I need your hand around mine. I'm lost without you.

Dear God,

thank You for
reminding us that we
need each other.

Help us to always
appreciate the fact
that You have placed
us together.

Amen.

How Do I Love Thee?

Tell me, O you whom I love, where you
feed your flock, where you make it rest at
noon.

SONG OF SOLOMON 1:7 NKJV

My Dear Husband,

I love so much about you. Some people count their
blessings to help them go to sleep. But sometimes
I think I might try to count how many things I
love about you—for that's a blessing in itself. For
starters, I love the feel of your touch when you stroke
my hair. And I love the twinkle in your eye when we
share a private joke. I love how you call me up sometimes
just to hear my voice.

I love the strength of your arm wrapped securely
around my waist. I love how your hand envelops mine
as we walk along. I love the shape of your mouth as it
curves into a smile. I love the hearty sound of your laugh.
And like the song goes, "I love how you love me."

Dear God,

we ask You to help
make our love grow
like a well-watered
garden in springtime.

We ask that You'll
show us new ways to
share and
communicate our love
for each other.

Amen.

White hair is a crown of glory and is seen
most among the godly.

PROVERBS 16:31 TLB

My Dear Husband,

I love imagining you in the future. Sometimes I try to imagine us with white, wispy hair and parchment skin, our bodies slightly bent by the passing of years. And I wonder, will our love still be as fresh and young as it was on the day we repeated our wedding vows? I ponder how a fragile thing like love can endure the effects of time and years—how it can survive the hurts and misunderstandings which occur while living life. And I wonder if our passion can remain unhampered by aging?

To be honest, I sometimes see myself—the aging process already in motion—and I wonder, will you still love me as wrinkles deepen, age spots appear, and the inevitable pull of gravity makes my body sag? I need your assurance—tell me your love is here to stay.

Dear God,

we're all getting older.
Remind us that our
love for each other is
based on who we are
and not on how we
look.

Amen.

Distractions Come

I am sending you out as sheep among
wolves. Be as wary as serpents and
harmless as doves.

MATTHEW 10:16 TLB

My Dear Husband,

I bless you for focusing on our love. As we move through life, we are constantly bombarded with all kinds of distractions. They come in various shapes and forms—anything from a pesky phone call to demanding work projects, family crises, or the daily needs of those around us. And occasionally these distractions will try to steal our focus from our marriage and take us in a completely different direction. That's when we need to be on our guard.

So, let's agree together to prevent distractions from turning into divisions that would come between us and separate us. Let's carefully gauge which distractions have the painful potential to divide—and then let's learn to quickly step away.

Dear God,

help us to be wise as we navigate through life.

Give us discernment for the distracting dangers that would divide us in our marriage, and help us to obey.

Amen.

What Makes Me Tick

Thank you for making me so wonderfully
complex! It is amazing to think about. Your
workmanship is marvelous—and how well I
know it.

PSALM 139:14 TLB

My Dear Husband,

I bless you for trying to understand. It's true; we
women are complex creatures. Our emotions can
be subject to confusing hormonal influences and
unexpected mood swings. And sometimes we don't even
understand why we react the way we do. But perhaps
that's just part of our feminine mystique.

For it's true, I do rely on intuition and feelings more
than you do. And I realize that can be annoying to a guy
who sees life from an analytical point of view. You must
feel frustrated sometimes. I do too. So let's learn to appreciate our differing points-of-view and remember that
God meant for us to complement each other.

Dear God,

you certainly did create us to be different.

Help us to step beyond the frustrations of trying to figure everything out and learn to value one another.

Amen.

I will send you the Helper from the Father.
JOHN 15:26 NCV

My Dear Husband,

I see God shaping our relationship. I believe it happens regularly—as we move through our day, taking care of life's responsibilities, trying to do what's right, working to get ahead—it's God's touch on our lives. It's those delectable little moments when God quietly administers His wonderful gifts of grace, protection, mercy, or love into our everyday routine. Where would we be without God's touch? I wonder how many times we forget to even pause and take notice.

And I can see God's touch on our marriage too—ways that He has preserved and watched over us. It's amazing how He continually knits our hearts together, how He strengthens our love and even teaches us to forgive each other. So, let's take time to acknowledge Him.

Dear God,

we thank You and praise You for your faithful touch upon our lives.

Please, help us not to take Your love for granted.

We know our marriage is a gift from Your hand.

Amen.

When We Give Gifts

You are generous because of your faith.
And I am praying that you will really put
your generosity to work, for in so doing
you will come to an understanding of all
the good things we can do for Christ.

PHILEMON 1:6 NLT

My Dear Husband,

I bless you for your generosity. Isn't it a wonderful delight to be able to give someone a special gift? Something about the act of being generous really lifts my spirits and invigorates my heart. And I do believe that those of us fortunate enough to be on the giving end truly do attain the very best part of the blessing—for being able to give is better than to receive.

But I think the act of giving is even more fulfilling when we can do it together, as a couple. So let's talk about some ways we can give to others—ways we can share from the abundance of our lives, from our happiness, from our material wealth. And then let's live generously and enjoy the thrill of giving and blessing others.

Dear God,

teach us to live and to give with a generous spirit.

Show us those who are in need and ways we can bless them with the abundance You've so graciously poured into our lives.

Amen.

Quiet Moments

Be still, and know that I am God; I will be
exalted among the nations, I will be exalted
in the earth!

PSALM 46:10 NKJV

My Dear Husband,

I love being still with you. Sometimes my spirit
hungers for a special place of calm and peace
and quiet. And I long for an undisturbed portion
of time when I can simply bask in God's love and grace,
perhaps even enjoying a perfect slice of His beautiful
creation while I'm at it. And how I'd love to share some
of those delectable moments with you.

So, how about it? Can we plan for some pleasant
moments like that—just spending quiet time together,
doing something we both enjoy, but without the need to
fill up all the time and space with words or activity?
Instead, can we just allow our spirits an undisturbed,
peaceful interlude—just you and me and God?

Dear God,

show us some special
ways to spend quiet
time together.
Teach us to come to
You consistently, to
savor Your peace and
calm, and to be
refreshed together.

Amen.

We Both Change

Do not be conformed to this world, but be
transformed by the renewing of your
mind, so that you may prove what the will
of God is, that which is good and
acceptable and perfect.

ROMANS 12:2 NASB

My Dear Husband,

I bless you for accepting changes. It's as inevitable as the passing of time. For as the years steadily come and go, we change. But to stay the same would be to stagnate, to cease growing, and to eventually die. And so as life comes pushing at us from all angles, we do change; hopefully we become more like God. But some changes are hard to accept. Sometimes our human nature just wants everything to remain the same, but it doesn't.

So let's remember that change really is good. And as we watch each other changing and growing over the years, let's applaud these transitions, and let's welcome these new seasons of life. Let's learn to embrace change with wide-open arms.

Dear God,

You alone are changeless—Your love and grace and kindness remain constant throughout the ages.

But we are in continual transition.

We pray that You will change us to be more like You.

Amen.

You have ravished my heart, my lovely one,
my bride; I am overcome by one glance of
your eyes, by a single bead of your
necklace.

SONG OF SOLOMON 4:9 TLB

My Dear Husband,

I love being in your arms. Do you know how wonderful your arms feel around me? That cozy warmth, that reassuring strength, that stable security? How ye feet it feels when those feelings wrap themselves around me in the comforting arms of your love. There's something so indescribably delightful about the physical display of your affection.

It's a great way to start a day—or to end it. And, of course, it's welcome anytime in between. Your embrace reminds me of your constant love, and it warms my heart with feelings of safety and assurance. So, wrap your arms around me, my love, and remind me once again that you're here—that your love is steadfast and dependable. Warm me in your embrace.

Dear God,

thank You for the
capacity to warm and
strengthen one
another with
something as simple as
a hug.

Amen.

> The voice of my beloved! Look, he comes,
> leaping upon the mountains, bounding over
> the hills. My beloved is like a gazelle or a
> young stag.
>
> SONG OF SOLOMON 2:8-9 NRSV

My Dear Husband,

I've so many reasons to love you. Sometimes we get so busy and caught up in the hectic bustle of day-to-day living that, I must confess, I start to take our love for granted. But then, something will make me pause for a moment, and I'll consider all the things I really love about you. Let me try to put some of them into words.

I love the way you put others above yourself. And I love the way your heart wants to do what's right. I love the way you treat little children and animals and old people. I love the look in your eyes when you're sharing something that's important to you. But best of all, I must admit, I love that you are mine and I am yours.

Dear God,

there are many ways to express our love for one another.

But we ask that You would remind us to practice putting our feelings into words.

Amen.

Separate But One

Christ himself was like God in everything.
But he did not think that being equal with
God was something to be used for his own
benefit.

PHILIPPIANS 2:6 NCV

My Dear Husband,

I love the complexities of our relationship. Sometimes the "oneness" of marriage can seem confusing. I know we've been united in love; yet, without a doubt, we are still two very separate people. We still have very separate views, separate personalities, even separate gifts and abilities. Yet I know that God has made us one. We are one spiritually when we pray together. And we are one physically when we join together in our love for each other. What a great mystery this is.

Despite the ways we are "separate" from each other, God has also created us to become one in His sight. I appreciate the fact that you are so careful to respect my opinions and listen to my point of view. I just want you to know that it means a lot.

Dear God,

teach us to grow in
respect for our
differences yet
understand that you
see us as one.

It's an amazing miracle.

Amen.

Success is Highly Overrated

Lay not up for yourselves treasures upon
earth, where moth and rust doth corrupt,
and where thieves break through and steal:
But lay up for yourselves treasures in
heaven, where neither moth nor rust doth
corrupt, and where thieves do not break
through nor steal.

MATTHEW 6:19-20 KJV

My Dear Husband,

You are my favorite success story. Oh, I know how everyone makes a big deal about success these days. But I'm not sure about the way our culture defines that word. I often hear people speak of a successful life or of being successful. But so many times, it seems they are only referring to things like money, prestige, and accumulated wealth.

I'm glad that you are not a man who runs after the world's idea of success—that you would much rather see us living happily and enjoying our relationship. I am so pleased when I see you taking delight in simple everyday pleasures and appreciating the goodness of a life well lived. That, to me, is better than the common idea of success. Or perhaps that is the definition of success.

Dear God,

thank You for giving us the wisdom to appreciate real success and to recognize the things that really matter.

Help us to invest our time and energy in eternal things.

Amen.

What Means Most to Me

Instead, it should be that of your inner
self, the unfading beauty of a gentle and
quiet spirit, which is of great worth in
God's sight.

1 PETER 3:4 NIV

My Dear Husband,

I love that you care. I love it when I sense you want to do something really special—something smart and clever, something you think will make me happy. It's fun to wait for your little surprises to develop. I always enjoy seeing how you express your affection.

But I have to tell you that what means the most to me is when you take the time to really listen to what I'm thinking, what I'm concerned about, what I long for. When you sit down, undisturbed, and look into my eyes and honestly listen, it means so much. When you ask me how we can accomplish these things together, when you share your heart, when you take my hand and whisper that you love me, you are such a blessing to me.

Dear God,

the simple things mean
so much—
thoughtfulness, caring,
and pausing to really
listen.

Those are the qualities
we most appreciate in
You and in each other.

Amen.

True Riches

Those who want to be rich fall into
temptation and are trapped . . . For the
love of money is a root of all kinds of evil
But as for you . . . pursue righteousness,
godliness, faith, love, endurance, gentleness.

1 TIMOTHY 6:9-11 NRSV

My Dear Husband,

I bless you for your values. Have you noticed how people seem to be more and more consumed with the "big bucks"?—making a killing on Wall Street, winning the lottery, or dreaming of being a guest on the latest "millionaire" game show? I'm sure it's easy to get caught up in all the hullabaloo.

I want you to know how blessed I feel to have a husband who knows where true riches lie. I admire the way you are able to keep your eyes on those things that are real treasures. For earthly riches are only temporary, and sometimes they bring more problems than they solve, while God's treasures are truly fulfilling and last forever.

Dear God,

help us to keep our priorities in order when it comes to earthly wealth.

Show us how to focus our eyes and our energy on You and to seek out Your imperishable treasures.

Amen.

What Would I Do Without You?

Be careful then how you live, not as unwise
people but as wise, making the most of
the time.

EPHESIANS 5:15-16 NRSV

My Dear Husband,

I am so thankful for you. It's not something I like to think about, not something I ever want to experience. But sometimes, just for a flashing moment, I wonder: What would I ever do without you in my life? Where would I be if you were suddenly gone—taken in an instant? And the answer can feel so dismal, so lonely, so sad that I can hardly bear to think about it.

Of course, I do believe the Lord would sustain me. But I honestly feel that I would be totally lost without you in my life. I think I would be brokenhearted and lonely and—oh, so alone. And because of those feelings, I become more determined than ever to rejoice that you are with me now—to enjoy each and every day that we have together.

Dear God,

teach us to number
our days on earth
wisely, knowing that
any single one could be
our last.

Help us to live fully,
joyously, lovingly—and
without remorse.

Amen.

My Comfort Zone

Become complete. Be of good comfort, be
of one mind, live in peace; and the God of
love and peace will be with you.

2 CORINTHIANS 13:11 NKJV

My Dear Husband,

Being with you puts me at ease. You've heard people say that "everyone needs to step out of his or her comfort gone from time to time." And while I understand that concept in general, I must protest a little. For you are my comfort gone, my love. And I have no intention of stepping away.

I love feeling like I can step into your presence, your arms, your protection, your love—and experience a sense of safety and comfort. And I believe that God gave you to me, specifically, to be my comfort gone. It's just the right place for me. I hope you feel the same way about me. I hope you can step into my presence and feel at home, loved, safe. I say let's keep our comfort zones.

Dear God,

thank You for giving us the comfort zone of each other's arms. Thank You also for providing a comfort zone for us when we come to You.

Amen.

They will talk together about the glory of
your kingdom; they will celebrate examples
of your power. They will tell about your
mighty deeds and about the majesty and
glory of your reign.

PSALM 145:11-12 NLT

My Dear Husband,

I love those "first times" with you. Remember the
first time we met, our first date, the first time
you took me into your arms, our first tender kiss?
Let's see if we can create another new kind of first
together. Let's make some brand new moment—or at
least let's do something old in an entirely new and different way. In other words, let's make afresh memory
together.

Perhaps we can plan an excursion—a little getaway.
How would you feel about getting up early and quietly
holding hands as we watch the sun rise over the eastern
hills? Maybe we could dream up something totally goofy
and unexpected. But whatever it is, let's create something
fresh and new—something we both can enjoy and remember in the years to come.

Dear God,

thank You for the gift
of spontaneity.
Teach us to use it to
create new and
memorable moments
together.

Amen.

My Favorite Things

Then he crowns it all with green, lush
pastures in the wilderness; hillsides
blossom with joy. The pastures are filled
with flocks of sheep, and the valleys are
carpeted with grain. All the world shouts
with joy, and sings.

PSALM 65:11-13 TLB

My Dear Husband,

I bless you for our simple pleasures. It's the simple things that give me the most joy, my love—the everyday pleasures of a life well lived. You don't need to bring me roses or French perfume or tickets for a Caribbean cruise. Not that those things aren't lovely, but my favorite things are much more accessible and affordable—they're only a thought away.

I like snuggling together in bed for an extra few minutes before we both head off into our busy days and holding hands in the middle of a crowd of strangers. I just love sharing an intimate, candlelit conversation for two and walking together beneath a canopy of stars. These precious times with you are my favorite things.

Dear God,

thank You for giving us an appreciation for the simple pleasures of life.

Amen.

The Way You Walk

My beloved speaks and says to me: "Arise,
my love, my fair one, and come away; for
now the winter is past, the rain is over and
gone. The flowers appear on the earth;
the time of singing has come."

SONG OF SOLOMON 2:10-12 NRSV

My Dear Husband,

I love seeing you move through life. I can see you coming from a distance, and I know right away that it's you. For you have a certain, unmistakable gait that can only belong to you. And it's just one of those many things about you that I love so much. It's one of those unique qualities that is yours and yours alone. I'm so thankful that God made you just the way He did.

And it's the same way with your smile—it's a "one-of-a-kind, light-up-the-room, and light-up-my-heart" kind of smile. And there's the way you talk when you're enthused about something or the way that you tell a joke. I love the way you hold your head at a certain angle when you're thinking deeply. All these traits are undeniably you. And how I love them.

Dear God,

thank You for creating everyone so distinctly different.

We appreciate all the unique little things that You have placed in each of us.

They are the things that make us who we are.

Amen.

Whispers in the Night

His speech is most sweet, and he is
altogether desirable. This is my beloved
and this is my friend, O daughters of
Jerusalem.

SONG OF SOLOMON 5:16 NRSV

My Dear Husband,

I bless you for our midnight chats. Remember those times we had long conversations, late into the night? We knew that we might disturb others and so we tried to keep it quiet, talking in hushed, yet intense, tones. But all the same, we weren't willing to give up our discussions in exchange for slumber. We had too much to say and too much to share to relinquish those times for sleep.

I still long for those private little talks, those sweet whispers in the night, meant for our ears alone—the intimacy, the sharing, the trust, and the love. And that's what a good marriage is made of I'm sure. So, let's do it again. Let's talk in hushed tones, telling secrets, suppressing laughter—let's whisper in the dark.

Dear God,

thank You for the
intimacy of marriage
and the welcome fun
that comes with it.

Help us to continue to
build a solid foundation
of trust and to share
from the depths of
our hearts.

Amen.

Our Favorite Song

We praise you, Lord, for all your glorious
power. With music and singing we
celebrate your mighty acts.

PSALM 21:13 NLT

My Dear Husband,

Our love is like sweet music. Doesn't every couple have a special song? Perhaps it's a favorite tune that was popular when they first courted—or a sentimental number performed at their wedding—or even a recent song that holds some special meaning for both of them. What is ours, my love? Do we have one? Dt's remember the songs we used to enjoy together; and then let's listen to them again, and let's recall why they were significant back then. Or let's consider what they mean to us now.

And if we can't remember a specific song, then let's put our heads together and come up with one—a brand-new song. And let's make it our own—a milestone for the time we've spent together, a reminder of our romance, a token of our love.

Dear God,

music communicates in
ways that words fail.

Thank You for this
wonderful gift that
helps us express our
love for each other.

Amen.

You're My Soul Mate

I am overcome with joy because of your
unfailing love, for you have seen my
troubles, and you care about the anguish
of my soul. You have not handed me over
to my enemy but have set me in a safe
place.

PSALM 31:7-8 NLT

My Dear Husband,

I love the person deep inside of you. To understand the significance of a soul mate, perhaps
we should first consider the substance of the
soul—what it is made of. Our souls are the inner part of
us that understands the magnificence of creation, that
can relish a well-told tale or revel in a perfect symphony.
And we can give thanks to God for giving each of us a
unique soul.

If we're to be soul mates, my love, we need to share
some of these soulful pleasures. It can be as simple as
admiring a lovely sunset or as complex as understanding
a piece of classical literature. But whatever our souls
take pleasure in, let's take time to experience these things
together.

Dear God,

thank You for those things that thrill our souls: music, literature, art, and nature, just to name a few.

They enrich our lives and draw us closer together.

Amen.

Your heavenly Father will forgive you if
you forgive those who sin against you; but
if you refuse to forgive them, he will not
forgive you.

MATTHEW 6:14-15 TLB

My Dear Husband,

I bless you for overlooking my faults. Sure, I wish I were perfect, and I'll admit sometimes I might even act like I am (at least for a moment or two). But we both know that I'm not. We both know that in reality I'm human with all the flaws that go with it. And sometimes I just plain blow it. Whether it's from selfishness, busyness, or just ignorance, the truth is, I can make some pretty big mistakes.

It makes all the difference in the world, my love, that you are always so gracious, kind, forgiving, and supportive (okay, almost always). I feel like I can pick myself up, ask your forgiveness, and go on—and hopefully not blow it so badly the next time.

Dear God,

help us both to be
quick to support the
other when we blow it.

Teach us to be
gracious and forgiving.
as You are.

Show us how to lend a
hand to help the other
one up.

Amen.

> Unless the Lord builds the house, They labor in vain who build it; Unless the Lord guards the city, The watchman keeps awake in vain.

PSALM 127:1 NASB

My Dear Husband,

I delight in what we're becoming. Sometimes I lose sight of this thing that we're building together—this thing called love, home, and family. I know how I can get so caught up in the less-important details of daily living that I almost forget that you and I are actually constructing something amazingly big—something significant and hopefully something lasting.

I want our marriage, our family, our home to be like a city on a high hill—something that people can see from miles around and marvel at. I want our love to shine like a beacon of hope to all who witness it, reminding them that God is good and that grace is real. I want to build something that will continue even after we are gone.

Dear God,

we need Your help to build this thing. We need Your hands on our lives to make our marriage a monument to You—a symbol of Your love, Your grace, Your mercy, Your forgiveness.

Amen.

Open Hearts

As God's chosen people, holy and dearly
loved, clothe yourselves with compassion,
kindness, humility, gentleness and patience.
Bear with each other and forgive whatever
grievances you may have against one
another. Forgive as the Lord forgave you.

COLOSSIANS 3:12-13 NIV

My Dear Husband,

I love that your heart trusts me. What I long for more than anything in our marriage is to keep my heart open to you—and for you to do the same with me. But I know it's not easy to remain in this position of vulnerability—at least not continuously. Misunderstandings come and hurts happen; and before we know it; our hearts are closing up again.

But forgiveness and love can open a heart's closed door. And as we learn to trust each other more completely, we can reassure one another that our love is a safe place, a secure haven. And that's when our hearts open up, and we begin to share deeply.

Dear God,

help us to create a
relationship that's safe
and secure and
trustworthy.

Teach us to keep our
hearts open so that
our love can mature
and grow.

Amen.

I remember what the Lord did; I remember
the miracles you did long ago. I think about
all the things you did and consider your
deeds.

PSALM 77:11-12 NCV

My Dear Husband,

I bless you for those wonderful yesterdays. I remember the first time our eyes met in a look that said, "There's something going on here." I remember the rush that ran through me—the electricity in the air. I remember the first time you wrapped your hand around mine, the warmth, the security. I remember thinking I'd always be safe in your arms.

I remember the first time you wiped away my tears, holding me close and comforting me with your blanket of love. We have shared and gone through so much together—so many experiences, so many memories. Let's take time to remember these things together—to celebrate them once more.

Dear God,

what a long way we've come.

When we think of all we've gone through, the places we've been—both the rewarding and the trying—we're so thankful that we've had Your help and support all along the way.

Amen.

Planning Romance

> So I decided it was more important to
> enjoy life. The best that people can do
> here on earth is eat, drink, and enjoy life,
> because these joys will help them do the
> hard work God gives them here on earth.

ECCLESIASTES 8:15 NCV

My Dear Husband,

I love it when you make intimate plans. When we were young and freshly in love, it seemed that romance just happened. We didn't seem to go to a lot of trouble; just being together was enough. But we did make plans to be together—didn't we? I can remember sometimes it was all I could think about—you and me, together, walking, talking, laughing, sharing.

But times have changed, and life's a lot busier these days. And now it makes sense to plan for romance. I recognize the need to take time to schedule a date and make preparations for a feeling of romantic ambiance. And just because these moments don't "just happen" doesn't mean they're any less meaningful. In fact, like a well-choreographed ballet, they can be delightful.

Dear God,

teach us new ways to
bring creativity and
imagination into our
love.

Amen.

Our Sweet Secrets

How sweet is your love, my darling, my
bride. How much better it is than mere
wine. The perfume of your love is more
fragrant than all the richest spices.

SONG OF SOLOMON 4:10 TLB

My Dear Husband,

I love our private times together. I love knowing that I can trust you with my most intimate secrets and that these things will remain private—just a sweet confidence shared between the two of us. This level of trust is one of my favorite things about married life. Having someone I can safely trust and confide in is a precious gift. I love knowing you won't betray me or let me down.

I want you to know your secrets are just as safe with me. I want you to be secure in my ability to maintain a confidence. For we need to protect those private places in our relationship, places where no one else can enter. And we need to put our heads together and whisper without fear of being overheard. Then our trust will flourish and grow.

Dear God,

teach us each day to
develop listening ears,
understanding hearts,
and the ability to keep
a confidence.

Amen.

Let's Talk about Eternity

Love never fails. But where there are
prophecies, they will cease; where there
are tongues, they will be stilled; where
there is knowledge, it will pass away.

1 CORINTHIANS 13:8 NIV

My Dear Husband,

I want our love to go on and on. We have promised
that our love will live forever—or at least "until
death do us part." But I realize our earthbound
minds don't understand the concept of forever all that
well.

Only God can comprehend such things. And sometimes I wonder what it will be like in the hereafter. What
will become of our love?

That's when I realize, all I can do is trust God—
believing that He's the One who has bound our hearts
together; and only He knows what will happen to our
relationship in light of eternity. But this one thing I
know; I believe in my heart our love will continue. In
some shape or form, I feel certain it will go on, because
real love cannot die.

Dear God,

some things are too great for our human, finite minds to understand—things like, what happens to our relationship when there's no such thing as marriage in Heaven.

But we know we can trust You with these questions.

And like little children, we know You know best.

Amen.

Our Love Complete

Being confident of this, that he who began
a good work in you will carry it on to
completion until the day of Christ Jesus.

PHILIPPIANS 1:6 NIV

My Dear Husband,

I delight in how our love grows stronger. Even if I attempted to love you with everything within me, I realize even that would not be a complete and perfect love. For I am only human and cannot help but make mistakes. My love; though sincere, can often fall short—missing the mark or stopping too soon. But I believe God can complete my love. He can enable me to go the extra step and love you selflessly and with my whole heart.

I want to learn to let God love through me like this. I want to become all that I can be in our marriage—to be kinder, more loving, more generous in our relationship. But I know it will take time, commitment, and, most of all, God, to make my love for you complete.

Dear God,

You've begun a good work in our marriage; You've planted Your seeds of love in our hearts.

But we realize that only You can bring our love to a place of completion.

And we know it's a lifelong process.

We pray that You'll help us to cooperate with Your plan.

Amen.

A Shared Vision

Patient endurance is what you need now,
so you will continue to do God's will. Then
you will receive all that he has promised.

HEBREWS 10:36 NLT

My Dear Husband,

I love it when we're spiritually united. As our love and relationship grow, I hope we can begin to share a vision for what our Father God would have us do together. For I believe He brought us together for a special reason, something beyond our own personal fulfillment and delight (although we enjoy those things too!). And I look forward to our serving God, side by side, in some unique way.

I long to see God utilize our relationship to touch others. I desire that our marriage might become an outreach of love and kindness to those around us. For when our cup is so full, how can we hold back the richness of blessings? How can we keep all God's grace and goodness to ourselves? For I know, as we share, we shall also receive.

Dear God,

we pray You'll give us a clear vision of what You'd like to do in our lives. Show us ways You can bless others through our relationship.

Pour Yourself through us and onto others.

Amen.

Surely goodness and mercy shall follow me
All the days of my life; And I will dwell in
the house of the Lord. Forever.

PSALM 23:6 NKJV

My Dear Husband,

I will love you forever and ever. Although we don't fully understand the complexities of what our relationship will be when we step into the grandeur and majesty of our heavenly home, I do believe we'll be there together. I do believe that you, my husband, my closest earthly friend, will still be by my side, holding my hand in yours. I want us to be together forever.

I want to stand by your side as we gaze in wide-eyed wonder upon those heavenly gates. I want to walk with you as we travel those glimmering streets of gold. I want to bow down next to you, as we worship the King of all kings. And I firmly believe that our union will remain as strong—yes, even stronger—than it is here on earth.

Dear God,

thank You for bringing
us together for this
earthly pilgrimage
called life.

We look forward to
spending eternity
getting to know You
better.

Amen.

References

If you have enjoyed this book, you will also enjoy
other gift books available online:

Daily Blessings for My Wife
God's Little Devotional Book for Couples
Quiet Moments with God for Couples
If I Really Wanted to Have a Great Marriage, I Would . . .

If this book has impacted your life, we would love to
hear from you.
Please contact us at info@honorbooks.com